THE LAWS OF HUMAN BEHAVIOR

Understanding the Laws That Shape Our Thoughts, Actions, and the Complexities of Human Behavior and Decision-Making

Fanny Hinton

Copyright

The Laws Of Human Behavior
Fanny Hinton

Table of Contents

The Laws Of Human Behavior
Fanny Hinton

Author's Note

Dear Readers,

I am excited to present my book, "The Laws of Human Behavior." This book is the culmination of years of dedicated research, study, and passion for unraveling human nature. Within these pages, I aim to share valuable insights into the principles and concepts governing human behavior. Drawing on my expertise in psychology, sociology, and neuroscience, I strive to provide a comprehensive examination of how and why we behave as we do.

"The Laws of Human Behavior" explores various facets of human psychology, motivation, social dynamics, cognitive processes, and the influence of both environment and individual differences. By grasping these fundamental principles, we can achieve a deeper understanding of ourselves and others, empowering us to navigate our personal and professional lives more insightfully and effectively.

My objective with this book is not only to impart theoretical knowledge but also to offer practical applications and strategies for personal growth and development. I firmly believe that understanding human behavior is a potent tool for self-improvement, fostering healthy relationships, and attaining success in diverse areas of life. I am honored to guide you on this journey of exploration and discovery.

It is my sincere wish that "The Laws of Human Behavior" serves as a valuable resource, aiding you in unlocking your full potential and navigating the complexities of human interactions with confidence and understanding. Thank you for embarking on this adventure with me. I encourage you to delve into the pages of this book, ponder its insights, and apply its

principles to your own life. Together, let us delve into the fascinating realm of human behavior and uncover the laws that shape our existence.

With gratitude,
Fanny Hinton

Introduction to Human Behavior Laws

Are you ready to embark on an enriching exploration of the intricacies of human behavior? Join us on this captivating journey as we uncover the foundational principles that shape our thoughts, feelings, and actions, delving deep into the complex tapestry of the human mind and spirit.

In this comprehensive guide, we will not only unveil the fundamental laws governing human behavior but also navigate through the vast terrain of human psychology, motivation, cognition, social dynamics, and individual differences. Through a meticulous blend of key concepts, theoretical frameworks, and real-life case studies, we aim to provide you with a nuanced understanding of the multifaceted aspects of human behavior.

Furthermore, we will equip you with practical strategies, actionable advice, and transformative exercises designed to help you apply these principles in your daily life. Whether you seek personal growth, enhanced relationships, or professional success, this book serves as a roadmap to empower you with the knowledge and tools needed to navigate the complexities of human interactions with confidence and insight.

Moreover, we will explore the fascinating interplay between nature and nurture, the impact of societal influences, and the role of individual agency in shaping behavior. By unraveling these layers, you will gain a deeper appreciation for the richness and diversity of human experience, fostering empathy, understanding, and connection in your interactions with others.

As you immerse yourself in this journey of discovery, we encourage you to reflect, engage, and apply the insights gained, transforming knowledge into meaningful action. Together, let us embark on this transformative odyssey, unlocking the secrets of human behavior and awakening the immense potential that resides within each of us.

The Laws Of Human Behavior
Fanny Hinton

Chapter 1

The Nature of Human Behavior

The nature of human behavior is a fascinating and multifaceted topic that has intrigued researchers, psychologists, philosophers, and scholars for centuries. It is very complex and influenced by a combination of biological, psychological, social, and environmental factors.

It encompasses a wide range of actions, thoughts, emotions, and motivations that individuals exhibit in various contexts and situations. Understanding human behavior involves studying cognitive processes, emotions, motivations, social interactions, cultural influences, and individual differences. It's essential to approach the study of human behavior with a holistic perspective, considering the interplay of internal and external factors that shape and influence behavior. Let's delve into each of these aspects to gain a deeper understanding:

Biological Influences: Human behavior is significantly influenced by biological factors, including genetics, brain structure, neurochemistry, and hormonal influences. Genetic predispositions can play a role in personality traits, cognitive abilities, and susceptibility to certain mental health conditions. Brain structure and neurotransmitter levels can affect mood regulation, decision-making processes, and emotional responses.

Psychological Processes: Cognitive processes, such as perception, memory, attention, reasoning, and problem-solving, shape how individuals interpret and respond to stimuli in their environment. Emotions, including happiness, sadness, anger, fear, and disgust, influence behavior by serving as motivational cues and guiding decision-making processes. Motivation, both intrinsic (internal desires and goals) and extrinsic (external rewards or consequences), plays a crucial role in driving behavior.

Social and Environmental Influences: Human behavior is also shaped by social and environmental factors. Social interactions, cultural norms, societal expectations, family dynamics, peer influences, and environmental conditions all contribute to the way individuals behave. Social learning theories, such as Bandura's social cognitive theory, highlight the importance of observing and imitating others in shaping behavior.

Developmental Factors: Human behavior evolves over the lifespan, from infancy through childhood, adolescence, adulthood, and old age. Developmental factors, such as attachment styles, identity formation, moral development, and cognitive maturation, influence behavior at different stages of life. The nature-nurture debate considers the interplay between innate biological tendencies and environmental experiences in shaping behavior.

Individual Differences: Each person is unique, and individual differences play a significant role in human behavior. Personality traits, temperament, strengths, weaknesses, values, beliefs, and life experiences contribute to variations in behavior among individuals. Understanding these individual differences is essential for appreciating the diversity and complexity of human behavior.

Complexity and Interactions: Human behavior is inherently complex and often influenced by multiple factors simultaneously. For example, a person's behavior in a social setting may be influenced by their biological predispositions, past experiences, cultural background, current mood, social norms, and interpersonal dynamics. Studying human behavior requires examining these interactions and understanding the context in which behavior occurs.

Adaptation and Change: Human behavior is adaptive, meaning that individuals adjust their behavior based on feedback, learning experiences, and changing circumstances. Behavior can also change over time due to personal growth, education, therapy, or exposure to new environments. Understanding the mechanisms of behavior change is crucial for interventions aimed at promoting positive behavior or addressing problematic behavior.

The Nature of Human Behavior is a profound exploration into the intricate and multifaceted aspects that define human actions, reactions, and interactions.

Chapter 2

Behavior Change and Personal Growth

Behavior Change and Personal Growth" delves into the intricate dynamics of transforming behaviors and nurturing personal development. It begins by acknowledging the multi-stage nature of behavior change, recognizing that it involves a journey from awareness to action and maintenance. This journey entails understanding one's current behaviors, setting clear and achievable goals, implementing strategies for change, and sustaining those changes over time.

Central to this process is the concept of self-awareness. Individuals must first become aware of their behaviors, habits, and thought patterns to initiate meaningful change. Self-awareness enables them to identify areas for improvement, recognize triggers and obstacles, and understand the impact of their actions on themselves and others.

Self-reflection complements self-awareness by providing a structured way to evaluate one's experiences and responses. It encourages individuals to examine their beliefs, values, and motivations, fostering a deeper understanding of themselves and their goals. Through self-reflection, people can learn from past experiences, make informed decisions, and chart a path toward personal growth.

Strategies for changing habits play a crucial role in behavior change and personal growth. These strategies encompass a range of techniques, from setting SMART (Specific, Measurable, Achievable, Relevant, Time-bound) goals to using positive reinforcement, visualization, and habit replacement. By implementing effective strategies, individuals can break free from old habits, adopt healthier behaviors, and cultivate a positive mindset conducive to growth.

Personal growth encompasses various dimensions, including intellectual, emotional, social, and spiritual development. It involves continuous learning, embracing challenges, and seeking opportunities for self-improvement. Building resilience and adaptability are key aspects of personal growth, enabling individuals to navigate life's ups and downs with grace and determination.

Healthy relationships are another cornerstone of personal growth. Meaningful connections with others provide support, encouragement, and valuable feedback. They offer opportunities for collaboration, learning, and personal enrichment. Cultivating healthy relationships involves effective communication, empathy, mutual respect, and a willingness to invest time and effort in nurturing connections.

In essence, "Behavior Change and Personal Growth" explores the holistic journey of self-transformation. It equips individuals with the knowledge, skills, and mindset needed to initiate and sustain positive changes in behavior, cultivate personal resilience, foster meaningful relationships, and embark on a fulfilling path of continuous growth and self-discovery.

★ The Process of Behavior Change

The process of behavior change is a dynamic journey that involves several key stages. It begins with the awareness of a need or desire to change a particular behavior and progresses through planning, action, and maintenance. Let's explore each stage in more detail:

Awareness: The first step in behavior change is becoming aware of the behavior that one wants to change. This awareness can stem from various sources such as self-reflection, feedback from others, or external circumstances. It involves recognizing the impact of the behavior on oneself and others, as well as acknowledging the potential benefits of changing it.

Contemplation: After becoming aware of the need for change, individuals often enter a contemplative phase. During this stage, they weigh the pros and cons of changing the behavior, consider potential barriers or challenges, and assess their readiness to commit to change. It's a period of reflection and internal dialogue about the desired outcomes and the steps required to achieve them.

Preparation: Once the decision to change is made, individuals enter the preparation stage. This involves setting specific goals related to the behavior change, creating a plan of action, and gathering resources or support systems to facilitate the process. Preparation may include learning new skills, seeking guidance from experts or mentors, and establishing accountability mechanisms.

Action: The action stage is where the actual behavior change takes place. Individuals implement their plan, engage in new behaviors, and modify old habits. This stage requires consistent effort, perseverance, and the ability to overcome obstacles or setbacks. It's a time of active experimentation and learning as individuals navigate the challenges and rewards of change.

Maintenance: After successfully making changes to their behavior, individuals enter the maintenance stage. This phase involves sustaining the new behaviors over time, reinforcing positive habits, and preventing relapse into old patterns. Maintenance requires ongoing motivation, self-monitoring, and adaptive strategies to cope with potential triggers or temptations.

Termination or Relapse: In some models of behavior change, there is a stage of termination where the new behavior becomes fully integrated, and the old behavior is effectively extinguished. However, it's important to note that relapse can occur, especially during the early stages of change or during times of stress. Relapse is not a failure but an opportunity to learn, adjust strategies, and recommit to the change process.

Understanding the process of behavior change can empower individuals to navigate each stage effectively, anticipate challenges, celebrate successes, and stay motivated throughout their journey of personal growth and self-improvement.

★ Strategies for Changing Habits

Habits are powerful drivers of behavior, shaping our daily routines, actions, and decisions. Whether they are beneficial or detrimental, habits exert a profound influence on our lives. In this section, we delve into effective strategies for changing habits, empowering you to break free from undesirable patterns and cultivate positive behaviors.

Habits operate on autopilot, often without conscious awareness. They are formed through a cycle of cue, routine, and reward, creating neural pathways that reinforce the behavior over time. While some habits contribute to our well-being and productivity, others may hinder our progress and lead to negative outcomes.

Changing habits can be challenging due to their ingrained nature and the comfort they provide. It requires a combination of self-awareness, determination, and strategic approaches to override existing habits and establish new ones. However, with the right strategies and mindset, habit change is achievable and can lead to significant improvements in your life.

★ Effective Strategies for Habit Change

Changing habits requires a strategic approach that combines motivation, planning, and consistent effort. Here are some effective strategies for changing habits:

Identify Triggers: Start by identifying the triggers or cues that initiate the habit loop. Whether it's stress, boredom, or specific environmental cues, understanding the triggers helps you interrupt the cycle.

Replace with Positive Habits: Instead of focusing solely on eliminating a habit, channel your energy into replacing it with a positive alternative. For instance, if you're trying to cut down on screen time, replace it with reading, exercise, or hobbies that engage and fulfill you.

Set Clear Goals: Define clear and specific goals related to habit change. Break down larger goals into manageable steps and establish a timeline for achieving them. Clear goals provide direction and motivation, making it easier to stay focused and track progress.

Use Visual Cues: Create visual reminders or cues that reinforce your desired behaviors. This could include placing sticky notes in prominent locations, setting reminders on your phone or computer, or using a habit-tracking app. Visual cues serve as constant reminders of your goals and keep you accountable.

Practice Mindfulness: Cultivate mindfulness to increase awareness of your habits and reactions. Mindfulness involves paying attention to the present moment without judgment. By practicing mindfulness, you can identify triggers, observe your thoughts and emotions, and make conscious choices about your behaviors.

Modify the Environment: Make changes to your environment that support your desired habits. For example, if you want to eat healthier, stock your kitchen with nutritious foods and minimize the presence of unhealthy snacks. Creating an environment conducive to your goals makes it easier to maintain new habits.

Reward Progress: Celebrate small victories and milestones along the way. Rewarding yourself for progress reinforces positive behaviors and encourages continued effort. Rewards can be as simple as treating yourself to a favorite activity or acknowledging your achievements with positive self-talk.

Stay Consistent: Consistency is key to habit formation. Commit to practicing your desired habits regularly, even on challenging days. Consistent repetition helps solidify new behaviors and makes them more automatic over time.

Seek Support: Surround yourself with a supportive network of friends, family, or a mentor who can encourage and motivate you on your journey. Share your goals with them, seek their feedback, and lean on their support during moments of difficulty or temptation.

Practice Self-Compassion: Be kind and compassionate toward yourself throughout the habit change process. Understand that setbacks are normal and part of the learning experience. Instead of being harsh or critical, use setbacks as opportunities to learn, adjust your approach, and continue moving forward.

By incorporating these effective strategies into your approach to habit change, you can overcome challenges, break free from unwanted habits, and cultivate positive behaviors that enhance your well-being and success.

★ Self-Awareness and Self-Reflection

Self-awareness and self-reflection are powerful tools for personal growth and emotional well-being. Let's delve into each aspect and explore how they contribute to a deeper understanding of oneself and the world around us.

Self-awareness is the foundation of personal development. It involves the ability to introspectively understand our thoughts, emotions, behaviors, motivations, strengths, and weaknesses. When we are self-aware, we have a clearer perception of who we are, how we relate to others, and what drives us.

Self-reflection complements self-awareness by encouraging us to examine our experiences, actions, and decisions. It allows us to learn from past experiences, identify patterns, and make conscious choices aligned with our values and goals. Through self-reflection, we gain insights into our thought processes, emotions, and behaviors, leading to greater self-understanding and growth.

Developing self-awareness

Developing self-awareness involves various practices and techniques. Mindfulness, for instance, helps us become more present and attentive to our thoughts and feelings without judgment. Journaling allows us to record our thoughts and reflect on them later, gaining clarity and perspective. Seeking feedback from others also contributes to self-awareness by providing external perspectives and insights into our blind spots.

Self-awareness enables us to recognize patterns in our thoughts, emotions, and behaviors. By identifying recurring themes or habits, we can assess their impact on our well-being and relationships. For example, noticing patterns of negative self-talk or self-sabotaging behaviors allows us to address and change them for the better.

Emotional self-awareness involves recognizing and understanding our emotions. It allows us to manage emotions effectively, express ourselves authentically, and empathize with others. When we are emotionally self-aware, we can navigate challenging situations with composure and make decisions that align with our values and priorities.

Cognitive self-awareness pertains to understanding our thought processes, beliefs, biases, and cognitive tendencies. It involves questioning our assumptions, challenging cognitive distortions, and cultivating a growth mindset. By becoming aware of our cognitive patterns, we can enhance critical thinking, problem-solving skills, and decision-making abilities.

Engaging in self-reflection practices is essential for ongoing self-awareness and growth. Setting aside time for introspection, evaluating our progress towards goals, identifying strengths and areas for improvement, and aligning our actions with our values are all valuable self-reflection practices. These practices help us stay focused, motivated, and accountable on our personal development journey.

Seeking feedback from others is a valuable aspect of self-awareness and self-reflection. Constructive feedback provides valuable insights into how others perceive us, areas where we excel, and areas where we can improve. Being open to feedback and using it as a catalyst for self-improvement enhances our self-awareness and contributes to continuous growth.

Self-awareness and self-reflection contribute to enhancing our self-understanding. By exploring our values, beliefs, passions, and life purpose, we gain clarity on what matters most to us and how we want to live our lives. This deeper self-understanding guides our choices, goals, and actions, leading to a more fulfilling and meaningful existence.

Mindful living is a holistic approach that integrates self-awareness, self-reflection, and present-moment awareness. It involves being fully present in each moment, paying attention to our thoughts, emotions, sensations, and surroundings with openness and curiosity. Mindful living enhances our overall well-being, reduces stress, and fosters a deeper connection to ourselves and others.

Self-awareness and self-reflection are dynamic processes that empower us to understand ourselves more deeply, navigate life's challenges with resilience, and cultivate meaningful relationships. By embracing these practices, we embark on a journey of personal growth, self-discovery, and fulfillment.

★ Personal Growth and Development

Personal growth and development are profound experiences that empower people to unlock their complete capabilities, improve their wellness, and live satisfying lives. These transformative journeys enable individuals to realize their potential fully, leading to a more fulfilling and purpose-driven existence. Let's explore the key aspects and benefits of personal growth and development

Continuous Learning and Skill Development

Personal growth involves a commitment to continuous learning and skill development. This includes acquiring new knowledge, honing existing skills, and expanding our capabilities to adapt to changing environments and pursue our goals effectively.

Self-Discovery and Self-Actualization

Through personal growth, individuals embark on a journey of self-discovery, exploring their values, beliefs, strengths, and areas for improvement. This process of self-awareness leads to self-actualization, where individuals realize their true potential and strive to live authentically in alignment with their values and aspirations.

Emotional Intelligence and Self-Regulation

Personal growth nurtures emotional intelligence, which encompasses understanding and managing emotions effectively. It involves developing empathy, self-awareness, social skills, and emotional regulation, leading to healthier relationships, enhanced communication, and greater resilience in navigating life's challenges.

Adaptability and Flexibility

Growing personally involves cultivating adaptability and flexibility in response to change and adversity. It means embracing challenges as opportunities for growth, learning from setbacks, and adjusting our mindset and strategies to overcome obstacles and achieve our objectives.

Setting and Achieving Goals

Personal growth empowers individuals to set meaningful goals, clarify priorities, and create actionable plans to achieve them. Goal-setting provides direction, motivation, and a sense of purpose, guiding us towards personal and professional success and fulfillment.

Self-Improvement and Reflection

Engaging in self-improvement practices, such as self-reflection, feedback-seeking, and constructive self-criticism, is integral to personal growth. It involves evaluating our progress, identifying areas for development, and taking proactive steps to enhance our skills, knowledge, and overall well-being.

Resilience and Coping Skills

Developing resilience is a key aspect of personal growth, enabling individuals to bounce back from adversity, manage stress effectively, and maintain a positive outlook during challenging times. Building coping skills, such as problem-solving, emotional regulation, and seeking support, enhances our ability to navigate life's ups and downs with grace and resilience.

Healthy Habits and Self-Care

Personal growth includes fostering healthy habits and prioritizing self-care practices that nourish our physical, emotional, and mental well-being. This may involve regular exercise, adequate sleep, mindfulness practices, healthy eating habits, and nurturing positive relationships.

Empowerment and Confidence

As individuals grow personally, they experience increased empowerment and confidence in their abilities. They develop a sense of self-efficacy, belief in their potential, and a willingness to take on new challenges and opportunities with courage and determination.

Contribution and Impact

Personal growth extends beyond individual benefits to contributing positively to the world around us. It involves using our strengths, talents, and resources to make a meaningful impact, inspire others, and contribute to a more compassionate, resilient, and thriving community.

Embracing personal growth, helps individuals to unlock their potential, lead fulfilling lives, and make a positive difference in the world.

★ Building Healthy Relationships

Building healthy relationships is essential for our overall well-being and sense of fulfillment. Let's delve deeper into each aspect of fostering meaningful connections with others

Effective Communication and Active Listening

Effective communication involves more than just speaking; it's about expressing oneself clearly, honestly, and respectfully. It's also about actively listening to others with empathy and understanding. This means paying attention not only to what is being said but also to the emotions behind the words. Active listening fosters trust and openness in relationships because it shows that we value and respect the other person's perspective.

Empathy and Understanding

Empathy is the ability to put ourselves in someone else's shoes and understand their feelings and experiences. It's about being able to connect emotionally and show compassion. When we cultivate empathy in our relationships, we create deeper connections and strengthen our bonds with others. Understanding each other's perspectives, emotions, and experiences helps us navigate challenges and conflicts more effectively.

Respect and Boundaries

Respect is fundamental to healthy relationships. It involves honoring each other's boundaries, values, and autonomy. This means acknowledging and accepting individual differences, preferences, and choices. Respecting boundaries shows that we value the other person's needs and limits, which builds trust and fosters a sense of safety and security in the relationship.

Trust and Reliability

Trust is the foundation of every healthy relationship. It is built over time through consistent actions, honesty, and reliability. When we trust someone, we feel safe and secure in sharing our thoughts, feelings, and vulnerabilities. Trust also involves being dependable and keeping promises, which strengthens the bond between individuals and creates a sense of mutual understanding and support.

Conflict Resolution and Problem-Solving

Conflict is a natural part of any relationship, but how we handle it determines the health of the relationship. Healthy relationships excel in resolving conflicts constructively and respectfully. This involves listening to each other's perspectives, expressing emotions calmly, finding common ground, and seeking solutions that benefit both parties. Effective conflict resolution promotes understanding, growth, and deeper connections.

Support and Encouragement

Supporting each other emotionally, mentally, and physically is crucial in healthy relationships. It's about being there for each other during difficult times, offering encouragement and motivation, and celebrating successes together. This mutual support fosters a sense of belonging, strengthens the bond between individuals, and creates a positive and nurturing environment.

Appreciation and Gratitude

Expressing appreciation and gratitude is a powerful way to strengthen relationships. It involves acknowledging each other's efforts, qualities, and contributions. By recognizing and highlighting the positive aspects of the relationship, we create a culture of positivity, gratitude, and mutual respect. This fosters a deeper connection and a greater sense of fulfillment in the relationship.

Shared Values and Goals

Having shared values and goals creates a sense of alignment and purpose in relationships. It's about having common beliefs, interests, and aspirations that unite us and guide our actions. When individuals share common values and goals, they can collaborate effectively, support each other's growth, and work towards a shared vision. This sense of unity strengthens the bond and creates a supportive and fulfilling relationship.

Healthy Conflict Management

Handling conflicts in a healthy and constructive manner is essential for maintaining strong relationships. It involves avoiding blame and criticism, practicing active listening, and seeking win-win solutions. Healthy conflict management also includes being open to feedback, addressing issues calmly, and finding compromises that respect each other's needs and perspectives.

Continuous Growth and Nurturing

Maintaining healthy relationships requires ongoing effort, communication, and nurturing. It's about prioritizing the relationship, investing time and energy into it, and adapting to changes and challenges together. Continuous growth involves learning and growing together, supporting each other's personal development, and creating a fulfilling and resilient bond that lasts over time.

If you can invest on these elements as an individual, you can cultivate meaningful connections that bring joy, fulfillment, and resilience to their lives.

The Laws Of Human Behavior
Fanny Hinton

Chapter 3

The Law of Individual Differences

The Law of Individual Differences stands as a fundamental principle in psychology, highlighting the inherent uniqueness of each individual. This principle finds its roots in psychometrics, a field dedicated to measuring various psychological attributes. It acknowledges the vast spectrum of differences among people, encompassing aspects such as intelligence, personality traits, abilities, skills, interests, preferences, and learning modalities.

For instance, intelligence manifests diversely across individuals, with some showcasing proficiency in logical-mathematical reasoning, linguistic prowess, spatial cognition, musical aptitude, or interpersonal adeptness. Similarly, personalities are a mosaic of traits like extraversion, agreeableness, conscientiousness, neuroticism, and openness, influencing how individuals engage with their environment. Moreover, individuals exhibit a multitude of abilities and skills across different domains, spanning artistic talents, athletic abilities, problem-solving capacities, and leadership acumen.

Furthermore, each person harbors distinct interests and preferences, whether in the realms of arts, sciences, literature, sports, or other pursuits. Additionally, individuals adopt varying learning styles, impacting their preferred methods of acquiring and assimilating information. Visual learners may thrive with visual aids, auditory learners prefer verbal explanations, and kinesthetic learners excel through hands-on experiences.

The Law of Individual Differences underscores the critical importance of acknowledging and embracing these diversities, particularly in domains like education, employment, and psychology. By recognizing and valuing individuals' unique attributes, tailored strategies can be devised to cater to their specific needs, enhance their performance, and bolster their overall well-being.

It's essential to note that this principle doesn't negate the existence of shared characteristics, commonalities, or general behavioral patterns among groups of people. Instead, it underscores the significance of appreciating both the similarities and distinctions that characterize the human experience.

★ Understanding Human Behavior

Gaining insight into human behavior is a multifaceted endeavor that draws from a myriad of disciplines, including psychology, sociology, anthropology, and neuroscience. It entails investigating the intricacies of how individuals perceive, think, feel, and act, as well as the myriad factors that influence their conduct across diverse contexts. Researchers and scholars employ an array of theories, models, and research methodologies to unravel the complexities of human behavior.

Biological underpinnings, encompassing genetics, brain structure and function, and hormonal influences, significantly impact human behavior. Neuroscience elucidates the physiological mechanisms underpinning behavioral responses. Concurrently, internal cognitive processes such as thoughts, emotions, beliefs, motivations, and cognitive functions intricately mold behavior.

Psychological frameworks, spanning cognitive, behavioral, psychodynamic, and humanistic theories, provide systematic lenses for comprehending these cognitive and emotional factors. Moreover, social and cultural milieus wield substantial sway over human conduct. Social norms, cultural values, familial dynamics, peer relationships, societal expectations, and cultural customs collectively sculpt individuals' behavioral patterns.

Disciplines like social psychology and sociology dissect how interpersonal interactions and collective dynamics shape behavioral outcomes. Human behavior traverses through developmental trajectories across the lifespan, prompting scrutiny from developmental psychology. This field scrutinizes behavior metamorphoses from infancy through childhood, adolescence, adulthood, and geriatric stages, encompassing physical, cognitive, emotional, and social dimensions.

Environmental factors, encompassing socioeconomic status, educational opportunities, resource accessibility, neighborhood characteristics, and environmental circumstances, significantly mold behavior and impact outcomes. Moreover, individual variances, encapsulating personality attributes, intellectual capacities, skill sets, and life histories, intricately contribute to behavioral manifestations.

Scholars employ an arsenal of scientific methodologies, such as experimental designs, surveys, observational studies, interviews, and case analyses, to scrutinize human behavior intricately. A holistic and interdisciplinary lens integrating biological, psychological, social, and cultural perspectives is indispensable to unraveling the intricate tapestry of human behavior.

This holistic approach acknowledges the multifaceted nature of human beings and underscores the intricate interplay among diverse factors shaping individual and collective behaviors. By deciphering these multifaceted dynamics, we glean invaluable insights into human behavior, which can be harnessed across domains like psychology, education, business, healthcare, and social policy to foster positive outcomes.

★ Uniqueness and Variations in Human Behavior

Human behavior is incredibly varied and unique. While certain commonalities and trends exist, each person possesses distinct qualities, characteristics, and behaviors that distinguish them. This uniqueness stems from a blend of factors, including personality traits, cognitive abilities, aptitudes, and cultural backgrounds.

Furthermore, personal life narratives, encompassing experiences, upbringing, education, and socialization, contribute significantly to individual behavioral distinctiveness. Variations in behavior also arise from diverse influences like cultural norms, societal values, social expectations, contextual circumstances, and developmental stages.

Appreciating and comprehending the nuances and diversity in human behavior carries substantial implications. It facilitates tailored interventions, support structures, and educational methodologies tailored to individual needs. It also fosters effective communication and enables scientific exploration. Moreover, it cultivates societal and cultural awareness, nurturing empathy, tolerance, and inclusivity.

In essence, acknowledging and comprehending the uniqueness and diversity in human behavior celebrates individuality and enriches our understanding of human nature, fostering a more empathetic and inclusive society.

★ Personality Traits and Behavior Patterns

Personality traits and behavior patterns are intricately linked components of human psychology that significantly impact cognition, emotions, and actions. Personality traits encompass enduring patterns of thoughts, feelings, and behaviors unique to each person, remaining relatively stable over time and across various contexts.

Traits such as extraversion, conscientiousness, openness to experience, agreeableness, and neuroticism form the foundation of an individual's personality profile. For example, high extraversion is associated with sociability and enthusiasm in social settings, whereas high neuroticism may lead to heightened emotional reactivity and anxiety. These traits strongly influence behavioral tendencies and responses.

Personality traits are instrumental in predicting how individuals are likely to behave in diverse situations. A highly conscientious individual tends to exhibit organized, responsible, and thorough behaviors, while someone with openness to experience may display curiosity, creativity, and a readiness for novel experiences. Moreover, personality traits influence motivational drives, shaping individuals' goals, aspirations, and preferences.

Emotional reactions are another domain profoundly influenced by personality traits. Neuroticism or emotional stability dictates how individuals perceive, experience, and express emotions. Those high in neuroticism may demonstrate intense emotional reactions, while emotionally stable individuals exhibit calmness and resilience in challenging circumstances.

It's crucial to recognize that behavior patterns are not solely determined by personality traits but are also impacted by situational factors, cultural norms, social expectations, and personal experiences. The interplay between individual dispositions and external contexts, known as the person-situation interaction, underscores the complexity of behavior formation.

Understanding personality traits and behavior patterns holds significant implications. It aids in personal growth by fostering self-awareness, identifying strengths and areas for improvement, and aligning behavior with goals. In social contexts, this understanding cultivates empathy, enhances communication skills, and deepens comprehension of others' behaviors.

In professional settings, knowledge of personality traits informs recruitment, career development strategies, and the design of conducive work environments that accommodate diverse behavioral preferences. Psychological research delves into the intricate relationship between personality traits and behavior, constructing models to elucidate behavior patterns and exploring interactions with other psychological constructs.

In summary, personality traits exert a substantial influence on behavior patterns, contributing to consistency, predictability, motivational drives, and emotional responses. This awareness is instrumental for personal development, social interactions, occupational effectiveness, and advancing psychological understanding.

★ Cultural and Individual Influences

The impact of cultural and individual factors on human cognition, emotions, and behaviors across various situations is profound. Cultural influences, encompassing shared beliefs, values, norms, customs, and practices, significantly shape behavior formation. Social norms, derived from cultural contexts, delineate acceptable behaviors and guide interpersonal interactions.

Cultural values, embodying societal priorities and ideals, steer individuals' goals, decision-making processes, and behaviors. Early socialization instills cultural knowledge and norms, influencing attitudes, beliefs, and behaviors. Language and communication patterns, ingrained in cultural contexts, influence self-expression, worldview, and social interactions.

Concurrently, individual influences underscore the distinct qualities, traits, and life experiences of individuals. Personality traits, such as extraversion, openness, and conscientiousness, mold behavior patterns by impacting responses to stimuli, task approaches, and interpersonal dynamics. Life experiences, encompassing upbringing, education, relationships, and significant events, further diversify behaviors within cultural settings. Personal values, beliefs, and aspirations guide decision-making and prioritize actions.

Understanding the interplay between cultural and individual influences is pivotal for grasping human behavior comprehensively. Cultural factors establish societal norms, values, and socialization processes, shaping behavior frameworks and interaction patterns. They offer a context within which individuals evolve and engage. Conversely, individual influences recognize unique characteristics and experiences contributing to behavior diversity within cultural paradigms. This perspective acknowledges that individuals may manifest behavioral variations even within a shared cultural milieu due to inherent traits, experiences, and personal aspirations.

The equilibrium between cultural and individual influences varies among societies and individuals. Some cultures prioritize collective norms and conformity, while others accentuate individual autonomy and self-expression. Moreover, exposure to multicultural environments can lead to amalgamation of multiple cultural influences in individuals.

Acknowledging both cultural and individual influences is crucial for fostering cultural literacy, combating stereotypes, and appreciating the nuanced dynamics shaping human behavior. It champions inclusivity by valuing the diversity and distinctiveness of individuals within cultural frameworks. By navigating the interplay between these influences, a deeper understanding of human behavior emerges, facilitating empathetic interactions, cultural sensitivity, and effective communication.

Chapter 4

The Law of Conditioning

The Law of Conditioning serves as a foundational concept in psychology, elucidating how behavior undergoes shaping via a conditioning process. This learning mechanism entails establishing connections between stimuli and responses, culminating in behavioral alterations. Two primary forms of conditioning exist: classical and operant.

Classical conditioning, pioneered by Ivan Pavlov, centers on associating a neutral stimulus with an innate stimulus to evoke a response. Conversely, operant conditioning, pioneered by B.F. Skinner revolves around behavior modification via consequences like reinforcements and punishments.

The Principle of Conditioning underscores behavior's adaptability, highlighting the role of environmental stimuli and outcomes in behavior formation and maintenance. Leveraging conditioning principles enables individuals to alter behaviors across diverse domains like education, therapy, and skill acquisition.

Despite conditioning's significance in behavior, it's imperative to recognize other influencing factors, such as individual disparities, cognitive mechanisms, and biological inclinations. Nonetheless, the Principle of Conditioning furnishes invaluable insights into behavior modulation through associations and consequences, profoundly impacting psychology's landscape.

★ Classical Conditioning and Behavior Modification

Classical conditioning stands as a pivotal learning process conducive to instigating favorable alterations in behavior. Behavior modification, integral to refining specific behaviors, finds classical conditioning as an instrumental mechanism for achieving desired transformations. Employing classical conditioning within behavior modification necessitates a structured approach.

Initially, pinpointing and clearly defining the target behavior earmarks the commencement of this process. Subsequently, selecting a specific desired response or behavior becomes paramount as the desired outcome. Concurrently, identification of an unconditioned stimulus (UCS) capable of naturally eliciting the desired response is essential. Simultaneously, a neutral stimulus (NS) is earmarked, initially lacking the capacity to elicit the desired response but capable of association with the UCS.

Sequentially, the repeated pairing of the NS with the UCS ensues, culminating in the transformation of the NS into a conditioned stimulus (CS) capable of eliciting the desired response. This phase, known as acquisition, solidifies the association between the CS and the desired response. Subsequent reinforcement and fortification of the desired behavior occur through positive reinforcement once the conditioned response (CR) is attained. Positive reinforcement, such as praise or rewards, bolsters the connection between the CS and the desired behavior.

It's pivotal to acknowledge the possibility of generalization, where the CR can be provoked by stimuli akin to the CS. This phenomenon implies that the desired behavior can extend to other scenarios or stimuli resembling the initial conditioned stimulus.

Leveraging classical conditioning techniques within behavior modification yields efficacy across diverse realms like therapy and education.

Its application extends to conquering phobias, ameliorating anxiety, fostering desired learning behaviors, and beyond. However, the comprehensiveness of behavior modification may necessitate amalgamating classical conditioning with other techniques like operant conditioning or cognitive approaches. Furthermore, individual nuances, motivations, and cognitive elements warrant consideration when implementing behavior modification strategies rooted in classical conditioning.

In summation, classical conditioning emerges as a potent instrument within behavior modification, facilitating the association of stimuli with desired responses and engendering behavioral transformations.

★ Operant Conditioning and Reinforcement

Operant conditioning delineates a learning paradigm wherein behavior is shaped by its consequences, emphasizing the pivotal role of reinforcements and punishments in behavior modification. Reinforcements, particularly, play a pivotal role in this process by either bolstering or diminishing the likelihood of recurring behaviors.

The concept of reinforcement encompasses two distinct categories: positive reinforcement and negative reinforcement. Positive reinforcement entails introducing a desirable stimulus following a behavior, thereby augmenting the chances of that behavior recurring. For instance, praising a child upon completing homework or rewarding a dog for executing a trick exemplifies positive reinforcement. Conversely, negative reinforcement involves eliminating or evading an aversive stimulus post-behavior, consequently escalating the frequency of that behavior. An instance of negative reinforcement is employing an umbrella to evade rain, thus eliminating the unpleasant stimulus of getting wet.

Both positive and negative reinforcements emerge as effective instruments in behavior modification, fostering the repetition of desired behaviors by associating them with favorable outcomes. This association fosters a reinforcement loop over time, solidifying the behavior. However, the efficacy of reinforcement hinges on several factors, including timeliness, consistency, and alignment with the individual's needs and the behavior being targeted.

Moreover, the potency and efficacy of reinforcement techniques may vary based on individual differences and situational contexts. Operant conditioning and reinforcement strategies find practical utility across diverse domains like education, parenting, therapeutic interventions, and workplace behavior management. They serve as instrumental tools for behavior shaping, skill acquisition, habit formation, and the mitigation of undesirable behaviors.

Ethical considerations play a crucial role in the implementation of reinforcement techniques, necessitating responsible and respectful utilization aligned with individuals' needs, preferences, and motivations. Understanding these factors aids in selecting appropriate reinforcements and cultivating a supportive and conducive environment for behavior modification.

In essence, operant conditioning harnesses reinforcement as a potent mechanism for behavior modification, where positive reinforcement involves introducing a desirable stimulus, and negative reinforcement entails the removal of an aversive stimulus. Through reinforcement, individuals are incentivized to replicate desired behaviors, facilitating learning and behavior modification.

★ Learned Behaviors and Habit Formation

Learned behaviors and the formation of habits are intricately linked processes that encompass acquiring and solidifying behavior patterns through repeated experiences. These concepts are pivotal in comprehending how behaviors are learned, retained, and become automatic over time.

Acquiring learned behaviors entails various forms of learning, including classical conditioning, operant conditioning, observational learning, and social learning. Conversely, habit formation denotes the transformation of learned behaviors into automatic, habitual actions. Habits are triggered by specific cues or environmental stimuli and are reinforced by rewards or positive consequences.

The process of habit formation unfolds in several stages, commencing with acquisition, where behaviors are initially learned and practiced.

Subsequently, a cue-response association is established, linking specific cues with corresponding behaviors. Rewards and reinforcements play a crucial role in strengthening these associations, leading to habitual responses. Finally, automaticity sets in, where habits are executed almost effortlessly without conscious effort.

While habits can streamline routine tasks and conserve mental energy, they can also pose challenges if they are undesirable or unhealthy. Altering entrenched habits can be challenging due to their automatic nature. However, comprehending learned behaviors and habit formation holds significant value in diverse domains such as education, personal growth, and organizational settings.

Learned behaviors and habit formation are interwoven processes that enable individuals to acquire, automate, and perpetuate behavior patterns. An understanding of these processes empowers individuals and organizations to cultivate positive behaviors and attain desired outcomes.

Chapter 5

The Law of Reciprocity

The Law of Reciprocity, also termed the principle of Reciprocity, is a psychological and social concept that posits individuals tend to respond to others based on how they have been treated. It stems from the belief that people feel compelled to reciprocate favors, kindness, or positive actions they have received.

The Law of Reciprocity suggests that when one person does something favorable for another, the recipient feels a sense of obligation to return the favor. This can manifest in various ways, such as offering assistance, reciprocating a kindness, or providing something valuable in response. These reciprocal behaviors can arise from a sense of fairness, adherence to social norms, or the desire to maintain positive social bonds.

This principle is universal across cultures and societies and significantly impacts social dynamics. It influences behaviors like relationship building, cooperation, trust establishment, and even marketing tactics. Initiating positive actions often triggers reciprocal responses, fostering stronger social ties and mutually beneficial connections.

Reciprocity is evident in diverse contexts, including social interactions, professional networking, gift exchanges, and sales strategies. In social settings, reciprocal gestures contribute to nurturing and sustaining social connections. Professionally, individuals assist each other, share resources, and extend support, leading to a network of beneficial relationships. Gift-giving reflects reciprocity, as recipients feel compelled to reciprocate with a gift or favor. Businesses leverage reciprocity in marketing by offering incentives like free samples or discounts to evoke a sense of obligation and encourage future purchases.

However, reciprocity isn't solely driven by conscious calculations; societal norms, cultural values, and innate tendencies towards fairness and cooperation also influence reciprocal behaviors.

Understanding reciprocity aids in navigating social dynamics, strengthening relationships, and fostering goodwill. Engaging in positive actions often prompts reciprocal responses, fostering positive outcomes and enriching social connections.

★ Mutual Exchange and Social Interactions

Mutual exchange serves as a cornerstone of human interaction, encompassing a myriad of interchanges including the sharing of resources, favors, information, and support between individuals or groups. This fundamental aspect of social dynamics plays a pivotal role in shaping relationships, fostering cooperation, and contributing to the smooth functioning of societies.

At its essence, mutual exchange is instrumental in the creation and maintenance of social connections. Through the exchange of reciprocal actions, individuals establish and nurture trust, cooperation, and mutual understanding. Whether it involves acts of kindness, providing emotional support, sharing resources, or offering assistance when needed, these interactions contribute significantly to the development of robust and enduring relationships over time.

Furthermore, mutual exchange facilitates cooperation and collaboration among individuals or groups. By engaging in mutually beneficial exchanges, parties pool their resources, expertise, and capabilities to achieve common goals. This collaborative effort not only enhances outcomes but also cultivates a sense of interdependence, encouraging people to work together for collective success and shared achievements.

The principle of reciprocity is a fundamental aspect of mutual exchange. It underscores the idea that individuals feel a sense of obligation to reciprocate the kindness, favors, or support they have received from others. This reciprocal behavior, whether in the form of returning favors, extending assistance, or providing support, plays a crucial role in maintaining social equilibrium, fairness, and a sense of mutual obligation within communities.

Social norms and expectations also exert a significant influence on mutual exchange. Cultural and societal norms prescribe appropriate behaviors and guide the expectations surrounding reciprocal interactions. These norms not only shape how individuals engage in exchanges but also define the types of exchanges that are valued and recognized within specific cultural or community contexts.

Moreover, mutual exchange extends beyond interpersonal dynamics to encompass economic and trade relationships. In economic spheres, exchanges of goods, services, or financial resources are conducted based on mutual benefits and agreements. This form of mutual exchange serves as the backbone of economic systems, driving growth, development, and prosperity.

Effectively navigating mutual exchange requires effective communication, empathy, and understanding. It is influenced by a multitude of factors including social norms, cultural values, individual motivations, and the unique nature of relationships or contexts. Striking a balance between individual needs and collective well-being ensures that exchanges remain fair, respectful, and mutually beneficial for all parties involved.

Recognizing and appreciating the importance of mutual exchange in social interactions is essential for fostering positive relationships, building trust, and nurturing meaningful connections. Actively engaging in reciprocal exchanges not only strengthens social bonds but also contributes to the creation of a cohesive and harmonious social fabric characterized by cooperation, collaboration, and shared well-being.

★ Reciprocal Behavior and Relationships

Reciprocity is a fundamental element of relationships, where individuals engage in mutual exchanges of actions, gestures, and support. It is essential for the health and longevity of relationships, as it helps to build and maintain healthy and meaningful connections by fostering fairness, trust, and cooperation.

Reciprocity in relationships encompasses various forms. Emotional support involves being there for one another during difficult times, providing empathy, understanding, and a listening ear. Offering help and support when needed, whether it's with tasks, advice, or practical assistance, ensures that both individuals feel valued and supported in the relationship. Effective communication and active listening are also key components of reciprocal relationships.

Engaging in meaningful conversations, actively listening, and expressing genuine interest create a connection based on understanding and respect. Compromise and cooperation are also important, as willingness to compromise and collaborate, taking each other's perspectives into account, and finding mutually agreeable solutions foster a sense of fairness, equality, and shared decision-making. Celebrating each other's achievements is also a form of reciprocity, as it demonstrates support, encouragement, and a shared investment in each other's happiness and well-being.

It is important to approach reciprocity in relationships with a balanced and voluntary mindset, free from expectations or keeping score. Genuine reciprocity arises from a sincere desire to support, care for, and contribute to the well-being of the other person. Understanding the importance of reciprocal behavior in relationships helps individuals navigate their interactions, cultivate strong bonds, and foster healthy and fulfilling connections. By actively engaging in reciprocal behavior, individuals create a positive relationship dynamic that promotes trust, cooperation, and mutual growth.

★ Social Norms and Expectations

Social norms and expectations serve as fundamental guidelines that influence how individuals behave within a society or specific group, shaping their actions based on accepted standards and values. These norms establish a framework for understanding what behaviors are deemed appropriate, suitable, and valued in a particular cultural or communal setting. They play a crucial role in maintaining social order, fostering cooperation, and influencing individual conduct.

These norms encompass a wide range of behaviors, including etiquette, dress codes, communication styles, gender roles, and moral principles. They are instilled through socialization, starting from early childhood, and are reinforced through social interactions, either through positive reinforcement or negative consequences.

The expectations set by social norms define the standards for behavior in various contexts or situations, delineating how individuals are expected to behave, perform, or fulfill specific roles or obligations. These expectations can vary significantly across cultures, social groups, and environments. For example, the behavioral expectations in a formal workplace setting may differ from those in a religious ceremony or a casual gathering among friends.

Social norms and expectations impact behavior in several significant ways:

Regulating Behavior: They establish guidelines that govern and mold behavior, setting boundaries and delineating what is deemed appropriate or inappropriate. By adhering to these norms, individuals can navigate social interactions effectively and demonstrate conformity to accepted standards.

Social Cohesion: Social norms foster social cohesion by promoting shared values, beliefs, and behaviors within a community or society. They contribute to a sense of identity, common purpose, and belonging among group members, reinforcing social bonds and facilitating cooperation.

Social Control: These norms function as a form of social control, shaping behavior by instilling a fear of disapproval, criticism, or exclusion from the group. The desire for acceptance and approval motivates individuals to conform to social expectations to avoid negative repercussions.

Predictability and Stability: Social norms provide predictability and stability in social interactions by establishing common expectations and shared understandings. They enable individuals to anticipate the behavior of others and navigate social situations with confidence and efficacy.

It's crucial to recognize that social norms and expectations are dynamic and can evolve over time. Societies and cultures undergo changes that lead to the reevaluation and modification of these norms, influenced by cultural shifts, technological advancements, and societal progress.

However, social norms are not static or universal; they can vary across different cultural contexts, subcultures, and social groups. What may be considered normal or acceptable in one setting may differ in another, highlighting the contextual nature of social norms.

Understanding social norms and expectations is vital for effective communication, social integration, and cultural sensitivity. Adhering to these norms enables individuals to navigate social interactions successfully, establish rapport, and foster positive relationships within their respective communities.

Chapter 6

The Law of Social Influence

The concept known as the Law of Social Influence, or Social Influence Theory, revolves around the notion that individuals' thoughts, emotions, and behaviors are influenced by the presence and actions of others in their social environment. This law acknowledges the significant impact of social interactions in shaping an individual's beliefs, attitudes, and actions.

At its core, the Law of Social Influence encompasses various forms of social influence, including conformity, compliance, and obedience. These processes elucidate how individuals adjust their thoughts and behaviors to align with the expectations, norms, and authority figures prevalent in their surroundings.

Conformity involves altering one's attitudes, beliefs, and behaviors to mirror those of the majority or a specific group. This adjustment is often driven by the desire to belong, gain social acceptance, or perceive the majority's viewpoint as correct. Factors such as group size, consensus among group members, the expertise or status of individuals within the group, and the significance of the situation all contribute to the level of conformity observed.

Compliance, on the other hand, occurs when individuals respond affirmatively to direct requests or suggestions from others. This compliance may stem from societal norms, implicit or explicit social pressures, or a desire to avoid conflict or receive rewards. Various persuasive techniques, societal expectations, and the nature of the relationship between the requester and the individual influence the likelihood of compliance.

Obedience refers to the act of following commands or instructions issued by an authority figure. This obedience often arises from perceiving the authority figure as possessing legitimate authority, attributing responsibility to them for the outcomes, and fearing potential punishment or negative consequences. The renowned Milgram experiments, wherein participants were instructed to administer electric shocks to others, serve as a notable illustration of the potent influence of obedience to authority.

The Law of Social Influence underscores the profound impact of social elements and interactions on individual behavior. It underscores the sway of social norms, dynamics within groups, authority figures' influence, and the intrinsic human drive for social acceptance. These influences collectively mold individuals' beliefs, attitudes, and actions, frequently leading to manifestations of conformity, compliance, or obedience.

Comprehending the Law of Social Influence holds significant relevance across diverse domains such as psychology, sociology, marketing, and leadership. A nuanced understanding of how social factors wield influence over behavior aids individuals in navigating complex social scenarios, discerning persuasive tactics employed by others, and critically evaluating the impact of authority figures. Moreover, it underscores the importance of upholding individual autonomy, fostering critical thinking skills, and considering ethical ramifications when confronted with social influence dynamics.

★ Conformity and the Power of Group Influence

Conformity denotes individuals' inclination to align their thoughts, beliefs, and actions with the prevailing norms and expectations within a group setting. It constitutes a significant aspect of social psychology, highlighting the potent influence exerted by group dynamics on individual behavior.

The mechanism of group influence can induce conformity through diverse pathways. Normative social influence manifests when individuals conform to group norms to secure social acceptance, evade rejection, or assimilate into the group. Human beings inherently seek social validation, and the apprehension of potential exclusion or criticism from the group can prompt them to adopt the prevailing beliefs and behaviors.

Similarly, informational social influence arises when individuals conform because they perceive the group to possess valuable knowledge or insights. In contexts characterized by uncertainty or ambiguity, individuals may turn to the group for guidance and rely on the collective consensus to shape their own beliefs and conduct. The presence of group pressure, whether implicit or explicit, also contributes to conformity. The desire to maintain group harmony, avoid conflicts, or align with the majority viewpoint can generate a compelling urge to conform.

The magnitude of pressure to conform escalates with the size of the group, particularly when unanimity is perceived within the group. Additionally, instances of compliance and public conformity may occur, where individuals outwardly conform to circumvent disagreements or confrontations, even if their personal opinions or beliefs differ privately.

The influence wielded by group dynamics and conformity can yield both positive and negative outcomes. On one hand, conformity fosters social cohesion, collaborative efforts, and shared values within a group or society. It facilitates adherence to social norms and cultivates a sense of belongingness among individuals. Conversely, excessive conformity can stifle independent thinking, curtail creativity, and impede critical analysis. It may lead to the suppression of divergent viewpoints and perpetuation of detrimental or inequitable practices.

Understanding the dynamics of group influence and conformity holds paramount importance across various disciplines, including psychology, sociology, marketing, and leadership. Insight into the determinants of conformity enables individuals to engage in critical reflection regarding their own beliefs, make informed decisions, and resist pressures to conform when warranted. Furthermore, it underscores the significance of fostering environments conducive to independent thought, diverse perspectives, and respectful discourse within groups and societies.

★ Obedience and Authority

Obedience refers to the act of adhering to the directives, guidance, or mandates of an authoritative figure, irrespective of one's personal convictions or principles. It is evident that authority possesses a considerable sway over individual conduct. Individuals are inclined to obey when they perceive the authority figure as legitimate, which can be based on factors such as their status, position, expertise, or credentials.

This phenomenon was vividly illustrated in the Milgram experiments, where participants were instructed to administer electric shocks to others, even though it caused distress, solely because an authority figure instructed them to do so. The influence of social norms and expectations also contributes to obedience, as individuals may feel compelled to comply with authority figures due to societal norms, implicit anticipations, or apprehension of punishment or social censure.

Furthermore, individuals may experience a moral obligation to conform to the directives of an authority figure, believing that the authority figure bears ultimate responsibility for the repercussions of their actions. It is crucial to recognize that obedience to authority can yield both favorable and unfavorable outcomes. Therefore, comprehending the intricacies of obedience and authority is imperative to forestall abuses of power and foster a fairer and more ethical society.

★ Peer Pressure and Its Effects on Behavior

Peer pressure refers to the sway exerted by one's peers or social circle to conform to specific actions or beliefs. It holds significant influence over individuals' behaviors, often compelling them to act or think in certain ways to gain acceptance or avoid rejection from their peers.

The impact of peer pressure on behavior manifests in various forms. One such manifestation is conformity, wherein individuals adjust their conduct or beliefs to align with those of their peers. This inclination may stem from a desire to belong, garner approval, or evade exclusion. The apprehension of being judged or marginalized by the group can prompt individuals to conform to the prevailing opinion or engage in actions they might otherwise eschew.

Peer pressure can also precipitate risky behaviors, such as substance abuse, reckless driving, or participation in perilous activities. The quest for acceptance or the aspiration to appear "cool" within a peer cohort can override individual discernment, leading to choices with adverse repercussions.

Conversely, peer pressure can yield positive outcomes as well. When peers encourage each other to adopt healthy habits, pursue academic endeavors, or engage in altruistic endeavors, it can engender constructive behavior changes and personal development.

The influence of peer pressure extends to the formation of one's identity and self-perception. Adolescents, in particular, are highly susceptible to peer influence as they navigate the journey of identity development. They may embrace the attitudes, behaviors, and styles of their peer group to establish a sense of belonging and identity.

While peer pressure holds sway, individuals possess the capacity to resist its negative aspects. Cultivating assertiveness, honing critical thinking abilities, and nurturing a robust self-identity empower individuals to counter adverse peer influence and make decisions aligned with their values and beliefs.

The ramifications of peer pressure on behavior warrant attention from individuals, parents, educators, and communities alike. Creating a supportive and affirmative social milieu where individuals feel empowered to make independent choices, express their viewpoints, and withstand negative peer pressure is paramount. By fostering healthy relationships, fostering open communication, and nurturing self-assurance, individuals can navigate peer pressure in a manner conducive to their well-being and personal growth.

Chapter 7

The Law of Motivation

The Law of Motivation is a foundational principle that elucidates the driving forces behind human behavior and the factors that propel us to take specific actions. It delves into what ignites our behavior and propels us toward particular objectives. A profound grasp of the Law of Motivation enables us to harness our motivation effectively, guiding us toward desired outcomes.

Intrinsic and extrinsic motivations are two primary categories that influence our actions. Intrinsic motivation arises when we engage in activities because we find them inherently enjoyable or interesting. Conversely, extrinsic motivation occurs when we pursue tasks to attain external rewards or avoid negative consequences. Both types of motivation significantly impact our behaviors.

Motivation often springs from our needs and aspirations. Needs encompass fundamental psychological and physiological requirements, such as sustenance, shelter, safety, social connections, esteem, and self-actualization. Goals represent the outcomes we strive to achieve, driving us to fulfill our needs and actualize our aspirations.

Incentives and rewards also play a pivotal role in shaping motivation. These external stimuli incentivize us to undertake specific actions or pursue particular objectives. Rewards can manifest as tangible assets like money or possessions, or intangible rewards such as acknowledgment or a sense of accomplishment.

Expectancy theory posits that motivation is influenced by our beliefs regarding the relationship between effort, performance, and outcomes. Our motivation levels rise when we perceive that our endeavors will culminate in successful performance and desired results. Elements like self-efficacy, perceived control, and the value of anticipated outcomes exert considerable influence on motivation.

Establishing specific, challenging, and attainable goals can bolster motivation. Clear objectives prompt us to invest effort and persevere, even in challenging circumstances. Self-determination theory underscores the significance of autonomy, competence, and relatedness in nurturing intrinsic motivation and fostering ownership of our goals.

Motivation intertwines closely with emotions. Our emotional states, such as enthusiasm, joy, or fear, can either augment or hinder motivation levels. Positive emotions bolster motivation and engagement, while negative emotions may impede motivation. Cultivating emotional intelligence and regulation proves vital for effectively managing and harnessing motivation.

Leveraging the Law of Motivation entails comprehending and utilizing these principles to nurture and sustain motivation within ourselves and others. This involves aligning goals with personal values, offering intrinsic and extrinsic incentives, establishing clear expectations, promoting autonomy, and cultivating a supportive environment conducive to growth and accomplishment.

By grasping the Law of Motivation, we can discern the drivers of behavior, adapt motivational approaches, and create environments that enhance intrinsic motivation, self-determination, and goal achievement. This comprehension empowers us to cultivate a motivated mindset, unlock our full potential, and attain meaningful outcomes across various facets of life.

★ Intrinsic and Extrinsic Motivation

Intrinsic and extrinsic motivation represent two distinct yet interconnected drivers that propel individuals towards engaging in specific activities or pursuing particular objectives. These motivations vary in their origin and essence.

Intrinsic motivation stems from an internal source, driving individuals to partake in an activity or pursue a goal because of the inherent pleasure, enjoyment, or interest derived directly from the activity itself. This form of motivation is deeply personal, as individuals find the activity intrinsically rewarding. Examples of intrinsic motivation include engaging in hobbies, indulging in creative pursuits, or participating in activities that bring a sense of personal achievement or fulfillment. Intrinsic motivation is often associated with feelings of autonomy, competence, and self-determination, as individuals feel a sense of ownership and control over their actions and choices.

Conversely, extrinsic motivation revolves around external factors that incentivize individuals to engage in an activity or pursue a goal for the sake of external rewards or incentives, rather than the inherent enjoyment or interest in the activity. External motivators such as rewards, recognition, praise, financial gains, or tangible benefits drive individuals towards specific behaviors. For instance, working for a salary, studying to achieve good grades, or participating in a competition to win a prize are examples of extrinsic motivation. Extrinsic motivation relies on external stimuli to prompt and sustain behavioral engagement.

Both intrinsic and extrinsic motivations can coexist and influence behavior simultaneously, with individuals often exhibiting a blend of these motivations for different activities. The balance between intrinsic and extrinsic motivation can vary depending on the individual and the nature of the task or goal at hand. Research indicates that intrinsic motivation is correlated with higher levels of engagement, satisfaction, and sustained persistence in activities. When individuals are intrinsically motivated, they experience a sense of autonomy, mastery, and personal growth, which enhances their overall well-being and fulfillment. However, extrinsic motivation also holds value, particularly in situations where the inherent interest or motivation for a task may be lacking.

Understanding the interplay between intrinsic and extrinsic motivation is crucial in various contexts, including education, workplace environments, and personal goal-setting. Creating environments that nurture intrinsic motivation, where individuals feel a sense of autonomy, competence, and connection to the activity, can foster greater motivation, satisfaction, and long-term engagement.

★ Needs and Drives as Motivational Forces

Needs and drives are interconnected concepts that profoundly influence motivational dynamics. Let's take a closer look at each of them:

Needs

Needs represent fundamental physiological or psychological necessities crucial for maintaining well-being and achieving a state of equilibrium. Abraham Maslow's hierarchy of needs delineates various levels of needs, encompassing:

Physiological needs: These encompass basic survival requisites such as food, water, shelter, sleep, and other biological essentials.

Safety needs: These pertain to the need for physical and emotional security, stability, protection from harm, and a predictable environment.

Belongingness and love needs: This category relates to the desire for social connection, intimacy, friendship, and a sense of belonging within relationships and communities.
Esteem needs: These include the need for self-esteem, self-respect, recognition, achievement, and respect from others.

Self-actualization needs: Representing the highest level, these needs involve the pursuit of personal growth, fulfillment, and realizing one's full potential.

Meeting these needs is imperative for fostering individual well-being and motivation. Unmet needs can lead to discomfort or tension, prompting the emergence of drives.

Drives

Drives manifest as psychological or physiological tensions arising from unmet needs. They create a state of arousal or activation, motivating individuals to take actions aimed at reducing tension and restoring equilibrium.

Drives are often associated with specific goals or behaviors directed at fulfilling underlying needs.

For instance, hunger (a physiological need) generates a drive for food, prompting individuals to seek and consume food to alleviate hunger and restore bodily balance. Similarly, the need for social connection (belongingness and love) elicits a drive for forming relationships and seeking companionship.

Factors influencing drives include personal experiences, cultural norms, social expectations, and individual differences. Moreover, drives can interact with other motivational factors like intrinsic or extrinsic motivation, shaping behavior and goal-directed actions.

Understanding the interplay between needs and drives is pivotal in fields such as psychology, marketing, and human resources. By acknowledging and addressing underlying needs and drives, individuals and organizations can devise strategies to motivate behavior, enhance well-being, and achieve desired outcomes.

★ Goal Setting and Achievement

Goal setting and accomplishment are intimately intertwined activities that revolve around defining specific objectives and taking deliberate steps to attain them. Effective goal setting offers guidance, concentration, and motivation, while achieving goals instills a sense of fulfillment and contentment. Here are key aspects of goal setting and achievement:

Clarity and Precision: Goals should be unambiguous and well-defined, articulating precisely what you aim to achieve. Ambiguous or general goals can lead to confusion and a lack of purpose. For instance, rather than stating a goal like "improve fitness," a specific goal such as "complete a 5K race within three months" provides clarity and direction.

SMART Goals: The SMART framework is a widely-used approach to goal setting. SMART stands for Specific, Measurable, Achievable, Relevant, and Time-bound. This method ensures that goals are clearly outlined and feasible. Setting SMART goals enhances motivation and offers a structured path to success.

Breakdown of Goals: Large or long-term goals can appear daunting. Breaking them into smaller, manageable tasks or milestones makes them more attainable. Each completed step contributes to a sense of progress and encourages further advancement.

Commitment and Responsibility: Increasing the likelihood of goal achievement involves making a dedicated commitment and holding oneself accountable. This may entail sharing goals with others, seeking support from peers or mentors, or regularly assessing progress. External accountability fosters motivation and support.

Planning and Implementation: Simply setting goals without taking action is unlikely to yield results. Develop a comprehensive plan outlining specific actions, required resources, and timelines. Consistently take purposeful steps towards your goals. Adaptations and adjustments may be necessary, but consistent progress is key. Monitoring and Feedback: Regularly monitor progress and assess performance. Reflect on successes and areas needing improvement. Celebrate milestones and learn from setbacks. Adjust strategies based on feedback and insights gained.

Persistence and Resilience: Achieving goals often demands persistence and resilience in the face of challenges. Stay committed, maintain motivation, and cultivate a positive mindset. Embrace failures as opportunities for growth and development.

Acknowledging Achievements: Recognize and celebrate successes throughout the journey. Acknowledging progress and accomplishments reinforces motivation and boosts confidence, fueling further progress.

Goal setting is a dynamic process, and goals may evolve over time. Regularly review and adjust goals to align with changing priorities and aspirations. By setting meaningful goals, taking consistent action, and cultivating resilience, the likelihood of achieving desired outcomes increases significantly.

Chapter 8

The Law of Cognitive Dissonance

The Law of Cognitive Dissonance, formulated by Leon Festinger in the 1950s, delves into the intricate realm of human cognition, beliefs, and actions, shedding light on the psychological mechanisms that drive individuals to maintain harmony within themselves. At its core, cognitive dissonance arises when there is a perceived clash or discrepancy between two beliefs, attitudes, or between beliefs and actions. This discrepancy creates a state of discomfort or psychological tension, urging individuals to seek resolution and restore cognitive consistency.

One of the foundational principles of this law is cognitive inconsistency. This occurs when individuals confront conflicting thoughts, beliefs, or behaviors within themselves. For instance, someone who values healthy living but engages in unhealthy habits may experience cognitive dissonance due to the disparity between their beliefs and actions.

The experience of cognitive dissonance is not merely a passive discomfort; it acts as a motivational drive for individuals to reduce this dissonance and regain a sense of internal alignment. This motivational aspect propels individuals to employ various strategies aimed at resolving the conflict and restoring cognitive harmony.

These strategies for reducing cognitive dissonance encompass a range of approaches. One common strategy is behavior change, where individuals adjust their actions to align with their beliefs or attitudes. For example, if someone realizes that their behavior contradicts their values, such as being wasteful with resources despite valuing environmental conservation, they may take proactive steps to change their behavior, like adopting recycling practices or conserving energy.

Another strategy involves belief adjustment, where individuals modify their beliefs or attitudes to rationalize their behavior. For instance, a person who engages in a habit known to have negative consequences may downplay these consequences or convince themselves that the behavior has other benefits, thus reducing the discomfort of cognitive dissonance.

Additionally, individuals may seek out new information that supports their existing beliefs or attitudes while ignoring contradictory information. This selective exposure to information reinforces their pre-existing beliefs, contributing to cognitive consistency.

Minimizing the importance of the inconsistency is another strategy used to alleviate cognitive dissonance. By convincing themselves that the inconsistency is trivial or insignificant, individuals reduce the psychological discomfort associated with conflicting beliefs or actions.

Seeking social support is also a common strategy for reducing cognitive dissonance. Interacting with individuals who share similar beliefs or attitudes can validate one's own beliefs, providing a sense of reassurance and reducing the discomfort of cognitive dissonance.

The application of cognitive dissonance theory extends to various domains, including attitude change, persuasion, decision-making, and post-decision regret. In these contexts, the theory suggests that individuals are more inclined to adjust their attitudes or beliefs to align with their behavior rather than changing their behavior to match their attitudes, especially when faced with cognitive inconsistencies.

While the Law of Cognitive Dissonance is a theoretical framework, it offers valuable insights into human behavior and decision-making processes. It highlights the complex interplay between beliefs, attitudes, actions, and the strategies individuals employ to maintain cognitive consistency and alleviate the discomfort of cognitive dissonance.

★ Consistency and Inconsistencies in Behavior

Consistency and inconsistencies in behavior pertain to how individuals maintain stable behavioral patterns or demonstrate conflicting actions. The following points provide an in-depth understanding:

Consistency in Behavioral Patterns
Consistency in behavior reflects individuals' inclination to act in harmony with their beliefs, attitudes, values, or personality traits consistently across time and diverse contexts. This consistency fosters predictability and reliability in how individuals respond to specific

situations, making their actions more understandable and foreseeable.

Influential Factors on Consistency
Personality Traits: Individuals with enduring personality traits tend to exhibit consistent behavior regardless of the situation. For instance, someone with a conscientious personality trait is prone to consistently display organized and responsible conduct.
Core Values and Beliefs: Strongly held values and beliefs significantly contribute to behavioral consistency. Individuals deeply valuing honesty, for instance, are likely to consistently engage in truthful behaviors.

Self-Concept: Clarity and stability in self-concept play a vital role in behavioral consistency. Individuals with a clear self-identity align their actions with their perceived roles, aspirations, and identities.

External Influences: External factors such as social norms, situational cues, and environmental stimuli also impact behavioral consistency. Social pressures and situational contexts may prompt individuals to conform to expected behaviors, even if these behaviors diverge from their genuine attitudes or values.

Inconsistencies in Behavior

Inconsistencies in behavior encompass situations where individuals exhibit actions that contradict their beliefs, attitudes, values, or established behavioral patterns. These inconsistencies can stem from diverse factors such as situational contexts, conflicting motivations, cognitive dissonance, and personal development.

Addressing Inconsistencies
To manage inconsistencies in behavior, individuals can enhance self-awareness by examining the underlying causes contributing to these inconsistencies. This process involves introspection, reflection, and deliberate efforts to align actions with core values and beliefs. Strategies may be developed to bridge the gaps between intentions, attitudes, and actual

behavior, fostering a more coherent and congruent approach to actions.

Understanding Complexity

While consistency in behavior is typically viewed positively, it's crucial to acknowledge the complexity of human behavior influenced by internal and external dynamics. Factors like context, individual differences, and personal growth play significant roles in shaping behavioral consistency or inconsistencies. Therefore, evaluations of behavior should consider these multifaceted aspects to gain a comprehensive understanding.

★ Resolving Cognitive Dissonance

Navigating cognitive dissonance entails managing the discomfort stemming from conflicts between beliefs, attitudes, or behaviors. Employing a range of techniques can effectively address cognitive dissonance and restore internal harmony:

Behavioral Adaptation: Individuals often alleviate cognitive dissonance by adjusting their behavior to align with their beliefs or attitudes. For instance, someone valuing physical health may incorporate regular exercise into their routine, despite previous sedentary habits. This proactive approach bridges the gap between ideals and actions.

Attitude Reconciliation: Another strategy involves modifying beliefs or attitudes to rationalize behavior. Individuals may seek alternative explanations or justifications for their actions, finding ways to perceive certain behaviors as consistent with their core values. For example, a person who smokes but acknowledges health risks may justify their habit by focusing on stress relief or social connections gained from smoking.

Information Seeking: Seeking information that supports existing beliefs can reduce cognitive dissonance. People tend to gravitate towards sources or evidence that reinforce their views while dismissing conflicting information. This selective approach aims to reinforce established beliefs and minimize discomfort caused by contradictory data.

Minimization of Discrepancy: Downplaying the significance of inconsistencies is another common strategy. Individuals may convince themselves that the discrepancies are minor or insignificant, thereby reducing the psychological tension associated with cognitive dissonance. This strategy allows them to maintain a sense of coherence despite conflicting beliefs or actions.

Social Affirmation: Seeking validation from social circles that share similar beliefs or attitudes can ease cognitive dissonance. Interacting with like-minded individuals provides reassurance and validation, reinforcing one's existing views and diminishing the discomfort caused by internal conflicts.

Environmental Adjustment: Modifying the environment or situational context can help align beliefs, attitudes, and behaviors. For instance, individuals striving for healthier eating habits may reorganize their surroundings by stocking nutritious food options and minimizing access to unhealthy choices. This environmental change supports desired behaviors and reduces cognitive dissonance.

It's crucial to recognize that individuals may employ a combination of these strategies, and the effectiveness of each strategy can vary based on individual differences, personal values, cultural influences, and specific circumstances. Over time, individuals may adapt their approach as they navigate cognitive dissonance and work towards internal consistency and well-being.

★ Attitude Change and Behavior Modification

Attitude transformation and behavioral adjustment are intricately linked procedures involving the adjustment of one's beliefs, sentiments, and actions. While attitude change centers on reshaping thoughts and emotions regarding a specific subject or object, behavior modification concentrates on actively altering one's actions. Let's delve deeper into each concept:

Attitude Change

Attitudes encompass evaluations, opinions, or sentiments individuals hold towards people, objects, or ideas. Attitude transformation entails modifying or reshaping these attitudes, influenced by various factors like personal encounters, societal norms, cultural impacts, and information processing.

Several mechanisms facilitate attitude change

- Persuasion: Utilizing persuasive communication to alter attitudes via compelling arguments, emotional appeals, or credible information. This can occur through advertising, public initiatives, or interpersonal exchanges.

- Cognitive Dissonance: Addressing conflicts between attitudes, beliefs, or actions by adjusting attitudes to align with behaviors or beliefs, resolving cognitive dissonance.

- Social Influence: The attitudes and actions of others, particularly in social or group settings, can influence individual attitudes through conformity, social norms, and social comparisons.

Behavior Modification

Behavior modification entails purposefully adjusting one's conduct or behaviors, involving pinpointing specific behaviors, setting objectives, and implementing strategies to encourage desired behavior or diminish undesirable behavior. Drawing from psychological principles, behavior modification employs techniques like reinforcement, punishment, shaping, and modeling.

Behavior modification techniques encompass:
Positive Reinforcement: Employing rewards or positive outcomes to reinforce desired behavior, such as praising a child for completing homework to encourage consistent performance.

Negative Reinforcement: Reducing negative stimuli or aversive conditions to bolster desired behavior, like decreased stress and anxiety for regular studying.

Punishment: Applying negative consequences or aversive stimuli to discourage undesirable behavior, such as issuing speeding tickets to deter speeding.

Modeling: Observing and emulating others' behavior to promote desired behavior through positive role modeling.

Self-Monitoring: Tracking and monitoring one's behavior for increased self-awareness and facilitating behavior change, utilizing methods like journaling or self-reflection.

Attitude change and behavior modification are interconnected, with shifts in attitudes influencing behavior and vice versa. Internal factors like beliefs, values, and cognition, as well as external influences such as societal pressures and environmental cues, impact both processes. By comprehending these processes and employing suitable strategies, individuals can work towards aligning their attitudes and behaviors to accomplish personal and societal objectives.

Chapter 9

The Law of Perception

The Law of Perception delves into the intricate process through which individuals interpret and derive meaning from the sensory stimuli they encounter in their environment. Perception, a fundamental aspect of human cognition, encompasses the organization, interpretation, and meaningful understanding of sensory information. While there isn't a singular "Law of Perception," various principles and theories elucidate the mechanisms underlying this cognitive process. Here's a detailed exploration of key concepts related to the study of perception:

Gestalt Principles: These foundational principles in perceptual psychology propose that humans possess a natural inclination to perceive patterns, forms, and objects as integrated wholes rather than disjointed parts. Concepts such as proximity, which involves grouping objects that are close together; similarity, wherein similar features lead to grouping; closure, the tendency to mentally complete incomplete figures; and others contribute to how we organize and comprehend visual information.

Bottom-up Processing: This form of processing focuses on the initial analysis of sensory elements and their integration into a coherent perception. It starts with raw sensory data and progresses to higher-level processing, where individual features are pieced together to form a holistic perception.

Top-down Processing: In contrast, top-down processing involves using pre-existing knowledge, expectations, and contextual information to interpret and make sense of sensory input. Our prior experiences, beliefs, cultural background, and cognitive processes heavily influence how we perceive and interpret stimuli.

Perceptual Constancies: These refer to our tendency to perceive objects as relatively stable and unchanged despite variations in sensory input. Examples include size constancy, where we perceive an object's size as constant regardless of its distance from us, and color constancy, where we perceive an object's color as consistent under different lighting conditions.

Depth Perception: This vital aspect of perception enables us to perceive the spatial layout and three-dimensional aspects of our environment. Depth cues, both binocular (requiring input from both eyes) and monocular (available to one eye), play crucial roles in our perception of depth, distance, and spatial relationships.

Binocular cues like binocular disparity, which results from the slight differences in the images captured by each eye, provide information about depth and distance. Monocular cues, including relative size (larger objects appearing closer), linear perspective (parallel lines converging at a distance), texture gradient (details becoming less distinct with distance), and others, supplement our depth perception abilities.

This comprehensive understanding of perceptual processes underscores the complexity and subjectivity inherent in human perception. Factors such as cultural influences, attentional focus, individual experiences, and cognitive biases contribute to the diverse interpretations and nuances observed in perceptual experiences across individuals.

★ Sensation and Perception

Sensation and perception constitute interconnected processes essential for comprehending and interpreting our surroundings. Sensation denotes the initial detection and basic processing of sensory stimuli, while perception involves the intricate organization, interpretation, and meaningful assimilation of this sensory data. Here's a detailed breakdown of each process:

Sensation encompasses the activities of sensory organs detecting and receiving stimuli from the environment. It encompasses the conversion of physical stimuli into neural signals comprehensible to the brain. Sensory organs such as the eyes, ears, skin, nose, and taste buds play pivotal roles in gathering sensory input and transmitting it for further neural processing. For instance, light entering the eye undergoes conversion into electrical signals, forming the basis of visual information interpretation.

Perception constitutes the higher-level cognitive operations subsequent to sensation. It encapsulates the interpretation and structuring of sensory data to derive meaning from our environment. Perception is influenced by myriad factors including past experiences, knowledge, attentional focus, and expectations. It transcends mere stimulus detection by facilitating processes such as object recognition, understanding contextual significance, and emotional attribution. For example, perception enables us to identify a familiar face, discern its emotional expression, and associate it with a known individual.

The interplay between sensation and perception is intricately intertwined. Sensation furnishes raw sensory input to the brain, while perception refines and transforms this input into coherent, meaningful interpretations. The brain amalgamates sensory inputs from diverse sources and amalgamates them with existing cognitive schemas to construct our reality perception. These processes synergistically function to furnish us with a holistic understanding of our environment.

It's noteworthy that sensation and perception are susceptible to influences and inaccuracies. Various factors such as biases, cultural contexts, and individual disparities can affect our perception. Illusions and perceptual discrepancies serve as reminders that our perception may not always align with objective stimuli reality. Nevertheless, sensation and perception remain integral components shaping our daily experiences and facilitating our interactions with the external world.

★ Cognitive Biases and Perception

Cognitive biases are patterns of thinking or mental shortcuts that can affect our perception, judgment, and decision-making. These biases can lead to distortions, errors, or deviations from rational thinking, resulting in skewed interpretations of information. Here are some cognitive biases that can influence perception:

Confirmation Bias: This bias involves seeking, interpreting, and remembering information in a way that confirms our pre-existing beliefs or expectations. We may selectively perceive and focus on information that aligns with our views, while disregarding or downplaying contradictory evidence.

Availability Heuristic: The availability heuristic is a mental shortcut where we make judgments based on the ease with which examples or instances come to mind. If certain examples or instances readily come to mind, we may overestimate their frequency or significance.

Anchoring Bias: The anchoring bias occurs when we rely too heavily on an initial piece of information (the anchor) when making judgments or decisions. This anchor can bias subsequent perceptions and lead to an inadequate adjustment of our perceptions from the initial reference point.

Framing Effect: The framing effect refers to how the presentation or framing of information can influence our perception and decision-making. The way information is framed or presented can lead to different perceptions and choices, even if the underlying information is the same.

Selective Perception: Selective perception refers to the tendency to perceive and remember information that aligns with our existing beliefs, values, or expectations, while filtering out or distorting information that contradicts them.

These cognitive biases demonstrate how our perception can be influenced by mental shortcuts and ingrained patterns of thinking. They can lead to perceptual errors, inaccuracies, or skewed interpretations of information. Being aware of these biases can help us become more conscious of our cognitive tendencies and make more informed and objective judgments.

Cognitive biases are not necessarily negative. They often serve as mental shortcuts that help us process information quickly. However, they can also lead to flawed or biased perceptions if we are not aware of their influence. Being mindful of these biases can help us approach information with a more critical and balanced perspective.

★ Cultural Influences on Perception

Cultural influences play a significant role in shaping our perception and how we make sense of the world. Culture encompasses a broad spectrum of elements like shared beliefs, values, norms, customs, traditions, and language, all of which contribute to shaping our cognitive processes and perceptual experiences. Let's delve into the ways cultural influences impact perception:

Cultural Schema: Cultural schema refers to the mental framework or template individuals develop based on their cultural experiences. This framework includes shared knowledge, expectations, and assumptions about various aspects of life, such as social roles, relationships, and behaviors. Cultural schemas play a pivotal role in how we interpret and understand the sensory information we encounter.

Context and Social Norms: Culture shapes our comprehension of social norms, appropriate conduct, and acceptable ways of interacting with others. These norms influence how we perceive social cues, nonverbal communication, and appropriate responses in social settings. For instance, cultural variations in eye contact, personal space, and gestures lead to diverse interpretations and perceptions.

Language and Perception: Language, closely intertwined with culture, impacts perception by influencing how we categorize, label, and describe our surroundings. Different languages possess unique vocabulary, grammar, and conceptual systems, leading to variations in how individuals perceive and interpret their environment. For instance, cultures with nuanced color terms may have heightened sensitivity and discrimination in color perception compared to those with fewer color distinctions.

Cultural Values and Beliefs: Cultural values and beliefs shape our priorities, attitudes, and worldview, influencing what we perceive as important or desirable. For example, cultures emphasizing collectivism may prioritize group harmony and interdependence, impacting how individuals perceive and prioritize social interactions.

Perceptual Illusions: Cultural factors can influence perceptual illusions like the Muller-Lyer or Ponzo illusions. Studies demonstrate that individuals from diverse cultures, exposed to varying visual cues, may interpret these illusions differently. Cultural experiences and contexts influence how our perceptual systems process and interpret visual stimuli.

Cultural influences on perception are intricate and multifaceted. Diverse cultures harbor distinct worldviews, beliefs, and practices, leading to varied perceptual experiences.

However, it's crucial to avoid generalizations and stereotypes, recognizing that individuals within a culture may hold diverse perspectives. Understanding cultural influences fosters appreciation for human diversity, promoting intercultural understanding and empathy.

Chapter 10

The Law of Emotion

The Principle of Emotion is a foundational concept recognizing the profound and multifaceted role that emotions play in shaping human behavior and experiences. Emotions encompass intricate psychological and physiological responses triggered by a myriad of stimuli and situations, influencing our thoughts, perceptions, decisions, and actions in significant ways.

Emotions are not fleeting occurrences but rather complex phenomena that deeply impact how we navigate the world and interact with ourselves and others. They can range from motivating enthusiasm and passion to immobilizing fear or fostering feelings of joy, love, or sadness. Understanding the nuances of the Principle of Emotion requires delving into several key aspects that shed light on the intricate nature of emotional experiences.

Firstly, emotions are instrumental in the decision-making process. They often act as powerful guides that can sway our perceptions and reasoning, leading us to make choices based on our emotional states rather than purely rational considerations. This aspect of emotions highlights the need for awareness and mindfulness to avoid impulsive or irrational decision-making driven solely by emotional reactions.

Secondly, the concept of emotional intelligence plays a crucial role in understanding and managing emotions effectively. Emotional intelligence encompasses a range of skills including self-awareness, self-regulation, social awareness, and relationship management.

Developing emotional intelligence enables individuals to recognize and understand their own emotions, regulate emotional responses, empathize with others, and navigate social interactions with greater empathy and effectiveness.

Moreover, emotions exhibit a contagious nature, spreading through social interactions and interpersonal dynamics. This phenomenon of emotional contagion underscores the interconnectedness of emotional experiences within social contexts. Being aware of emotional contagion can help individuals navigate social environments more adeptly, fostering positive emotional climates and enhancing social relationships.

Emotional regulation emerges as a fundamental skill in maintaining emotional balance and well-being. Emotions can sometimes become overwhelming or disruptive, affecting mental health and interpersonal relationships. Learning techniques such as self-soothing, mindfulness practices, and stress management strategies empowers individuals to regulate their emotions effectively, preventing them from negatively impacting behavior and relationships.

Additionally, cultural influences significantly shape the expression, interpretation, and regulation of emotions. Cultural norms, values, and beliefs play a pivotal role in determining how emotions are perceived, displayed, and managed within different cultural contexts. Awareness of cultural variations in emotional expression fosters cross-cultural understanding, empathy, and respectful communication.

In essence, the Principle of Emotion underscores the importance of acknowledging, understanding, and harnessing the power of emotions in navigating life's complexities. Emotions are not merely fleeting experiences but integral aspects of human existence that contribute to self-awareness, interpersonal connections, and overall well-being. Embracing emotions as valuable guides enables individuals to embark on a journey of self-discovery, meaningful connections, and personal growth, fostering authenticity and fulfillment in life's journey.

★ The Role of Emotions in Behavior

Emotions constitute a fundamental aspect of human behavior, serving as a potent influencer that molds our thoughts, choices, and behaviors. They function as a perceptual filter through which we interpret and engage with the world, shaping our experiences and reactions. A comprehensive understanding of the role of emotions in behavior offers profound insights into the intricacies of human nature.

Emotions serve as informative signals that provide valuable cues about our inner states and external environment. They serve as indicators of our needs, desires, and concerns, guiding us in navigating life's challenges. For instance, fear signals potential threats, prompting us to take protective measures, while joy and contentment signify positive experiences, encouraging us to seek similar sources of happiness.

The impact of emotions extends to our decision-making processes, influencing our preferences, biases, and priorities. Emotional attachments can sway our choices, often superseding logical reasoning. Recognizing this influence helps us make more balanced and rational decisions, considering both emotional and rational aspects.

Furthermore, emotions play a vital role in our social interactions and relationships, facilitating emotional expression and connection with others. Empathy and understanding stem from our ability to resonate with others' emotions, fostering deeper interpersonal bonds. Acknowledging and responding to emotions enhances our communication skills and strengthens interpersonal connections.

Emotions also serve as motivational drivers, propelling us towards goals and aspirations. Excitement fuels our drive to pursue new opportunities, while negative emotions like fear or disappointment can act as barriers to progress. Understanding the motivational aspects of emotions helps us channel them productively towards achieving our objectives.

Over time, chronic emotional experiences can shape our long-term behavior patterns and personality traits, influencing our overall well-being and outlook on life. Developing emotional intelligence and self-awareness enables us to manage emotions effectively, respond constructively, and align our actions with our values and aspirations.

Embracing and comprehending our emotional landscape empowers us to lead authentic, fulfilling lives, fostering personal growth, meaningful connections, and a deeper understanding of ourselves and others.

★ Emotion Regulation and Emotional Intelligence

Emotion regulation and emotional intelligence are pivotal concepts that offer insights into managing and understanding our emotions effectively. Emotion regulation entails the capacity to identify, comprehend, and skillfully handle both personal and others' emotions. This skill set encompasses various strategies and techniques enabling individuals to adaptively navigate and control their emotional responses. Conversely, emotional intelligence encompasses a broader scope, encompassing the ability to perceive, comprehend, manage, and leverage emotions adeptly in self-context and interpersonal dynamics.

When individuals possess high emotional intelligence, they exhibit heightened awareness of their emotional states and possess the tools to regulate them in constructive ways. These skills can be honed through introspection, practical application, and drawing lessons from life experiences. Emotion regulation tactics encompass cognitive reappraisal, expressive suppression, mindfulness practices, and proactive problem-solving. On the other hand, emotional intelligence encompasses facets like emotional self-awareness, proficient emotional management, empathetic understanding, and adept management of relationships.

By nurturing these competencies, individuals can create a positive ripple effect in their lives, fostering improved emotional well-being and fostering meaningful connections that positively impact others. The development of emotion regulation and emotional intelligence is an ongoing journey that necessitates attunement to one's emotions and a willingness to accept constructive feedback from others. Armed with these proficiencies, individuals can effectively manage their emotional responses, effectively communicate their needs, empathize with others' experiences, navigate conflicts amicably, and cultivate enriching interpersonal relationships.

★ Emotional Influences on Decision Making

Emotions exert a profound and multifaceted influence over our decision-making processes, challenging the traditional view that decisions are solely based on rationality. Extensive research has unveiled the intricate interplay between emotions and cognition, revealing emotions as pivotal drivers that often surpass logical reasoning in shaping our choices and actions. Delving into the nuanced dynamics of emotional influences on decision making offers profound insights into human behavior, cognition, and the complexities of choice.

At the core of emotional influences on decision making is the notion that emotions serve as potent guides, signaling our internal states and external environments. They act as intuitive navigators, providing valuable cues about our desires, fears, and preferences. For example, emotions like enthusiasm and optimism can signal positive opportunities, nudging us towards exploration and engagement. Conversely, emotions such as fear or anxiety can serve as warning signs, prompting caution and avoidance of potential risks.

One of the fascinating aspects of emotional influences on decision making is their role in shaping our cognitive biases and preferences. Positive emotions can create biases towards certain options or outcomes, leading to favoritism and preference-driven decisions. On the contrary, negative emotions can instigate biases against specific choices, influencing us to steer clear of perceived threats or undesirable outcomes. These emotional biases often operate beneath conscious awareness, subtly shaping our decision-making processes.

Furthermore, the framing and presentation of information play a pivotal role in evoking specific emotions that influence decisions. The way information is framed can trigger emotional responses that sway our choices. For instance, messages emphasizing potential losses may evoke fear or caution, leading to risk-averse decisions. Conversely, highlighting potential gains can evoke excitement or optimism, fostering a willingness to take risks.

The social and cultural context also significantly shapes emotional influences on decision making. Emotions are contagious within social networks, spreading through interactions and influencing collective decision-making processes. Cultural norms and values dictate emotional expressions and responses, further molding decision-making dynamics. Understanding these contextual factors is crucial in navigating decision making within diverse social and cultural landscapes.

While emotions play a dominant role in decision making, optimal decision-making strategies integrate emotional insights with rational analysis. Striking a balance between emotional intuition and logical reasoning allows for more nuanced and informed decisions. Cultivating emotional intelligence, fostering emotional regulation skills, and acknowledging the interplay between emotions and cognition are essential steps towards enhancing decision-making efficacy. By embracing emotional awareness and harnessing the power of emotions in decision making, individuals can navigate choices with greater clarity, adaptability, and authenticity.

The Laws Of Human Behavior
Fanny Hinton

Chapter 11

The Law of Reinforcement

The Law of Reinforcement is a foundational principle that underpins human behavior and the process of learning. It centers on the concept that behaviors are influenced by the consequences they lead to. Reinforcement, as defined by this law, involves strengthening behaviors by either providing positive outcomes or removing negative ones. Essentially, behaviors that result in positive consequences are more likely to recur, while those leading to negative consequences are less likely to be repeated. This law delineates two primary types of reinforcement: positive and negative reinforcement.

Positive reinforcement entails offering a desirable stimulus or reward following a behavior, thereby increasing the likelihood of that behavior recurring. For instance, praising a child for completing their homework reinforces the behavior of diligent studying. On the other hand, negative reinforcement involves eliminating an aversive stimulus or alleviating an unpleasant situation after a behavior, thereby reinforcing the behavior itself. An example is taking pain medication to alleviate discomfort, which reinforces the behavior of taking medication when in pain.

Both positive and negative reinforcement play pivotal roles in shaping behavior by forging associations between actions and their consequences, strengthening their connection over time. This process leads to the automated integration of reinforced behaviors into our repertoire of responses. The Law of Reinforcement also acknowledges the concept of punishment, where aversive consequences follow a behavior with the intent of reducing its recurrence.

When applying the principles of reinforcement, ethical considerations and individual well-being are paramount. Reinforcement strategies should promote positive behaviors, nurture intrinsic motivation, and cultivate supportive environments conducive to growth. It's crucial to recognize that the Law of Reinforcement operates within a broader framework of learning and behavior, with various factors influencing behavior beyond mere reinforcement. Factors such as individual differences, timing, and contextual nuances can impact the effectiveness of reinforcement or punishment.

Understanding the Law of Reinforcement offers valuable insights into how consequences mold behaviors. By leveraging this understanding, we can actively shape our own behavior and influence the behavior of others. Implementing effective reinforcement strategies allows us to encourage desired behaviors and discourage unwanted ones, making this principle applicable across diverse domains like education, parenting, workplace dynamics, and personal development.

★ Positive Reinforcement and Behavior Strengthening

Positive reinforcement is a potent strategy used to reinforce and mold behavior positively. It entails presenting a desirable stimulus or reward following a behavior, thereby increasing the likelihood of that behavior recurring in the future. Unlike punitive measures that discourage unwanted behaviors, positive reinforcement focuses on acknowledging and encouraging desired behaviors.

When implemented effectively, positive reinforcement acts as a motivator by strengthening the link between the behavior and the favorable outcome. By associating the behavior with a pleasant consequence, individuals are inclined to repeat the behavior, anticipating the rewarding experience.

Positive reinforcement manifests in various forms, tailored to individuals and contexts. It can encompass verbal commendations, acknowledgments, tangible rewards, privileges, or any positive stimulus meaningful to the person. For instance, a teacher praising a student for completing a challenging task reinforces their diligence and motivates them to persist. Similarly, an employer providing a bonus for meeting targets reinforces productivity and inspires employees to excel.

The efficacy of positive reinforcement lies in its capacity to foster positive associations and intrinsic motivation. It empowers individuals to develop a sense of competence, autonomy, and self-determination, acknowledging that their efforts yield positive results. Furthermore, positive reinforcement nurtures a conducive learning environment by accentuating strengths, boosting self-confidence, and fostering a growth-oriented mindset.

Positive reinforcement finds applicability across diverse domains such as education, parenting, organizational leadership, and personal growth. By leveraging positive reinforcement, individuals can reinforce desired behaviors, nurture motivation, and establish a supportive milieu conducive to growth and well-being.

However, the effectiveness of positive reinforcement hinges on several factors. Firstly, timely reinforcement is crucial, ensuring the reward follows the desired behavior promptly, reinforcing the connection between the behavior and the positive outcome. Secondly, the reinforcement must be meaningful and relevant to the individual, considering their unique preferences and needs for optimal impact.

★ Negative Reinforcement and Behavior Weakening

Negative reinforcement is a potent method employed to diminish or lessen behavior. It operates by eliminating or evading an unpleasant situation or stimulus after a behavior occurs, thereby augmenting the likelihood of reducing or avoiding that behavior in the future. Unlike punishment, which aims to curtail behavior through adverse consequences, negative reinforcement concentrates on eliminating or mitigating something unpleasant to reinforce behavior reduction.

When applied appropriately, negative reinforcement can serve as a compelling motivator by permitting individuals to evade or escape an unpleasant experience. The elimination of the aversive stimulus reinforces the behavior that led to its removal, making individuals more inclined to engage in that behavior again under similar circumstances.

Negative reinforcement manifests diversely depending on the context and individual inclinations. It could involve eliminating a bothersome task after completing a specific behavior, escaping a stressful scenario, or evading an unpleasant consequence by undertaking a particular action. For instance, a student might be incentivized to complete their homework early to avoid the stress and strain of last-minute cramming. Similarly, an employee might exert effort to meet a deadline to avert potential negative feedback or repercussions.

The potency of negative reinforcement lies in its ability to engender a sense of relief or avoidance of discomfort. Individuals learn that engaging in a certain behavior enables them to escape or avoid unpleasant experiences, thereby increasing the likelihood of repeating that behavior in the future to attain the desired outcome.

However, it is imperative to exercise ethical and responsible use of negative reinforcement. It should be employed to encourage behavior reduction without inducing fear, coercion, or harm. Establishing a supportive and secure environment is crucial to ensure the appropriate implementation of negative reinforcement and prevent any adverse effects on individuals' well-being or motivation.

Negative reinforcement should not be confused with punishment. While negative reinforcement aims to amplify behavior by eliminating an aversive stimulus, punishment seeks to diminish behavior by introducing an aversive stimulus. Negative reinforcement bolsters behavior, whereas punishment weakens behavior.

Nevertheless, it is vital to contemplate the ethical and suitable application of negative reinforcement, as solely relying on the removal of aversive stimuli may not always be the most effective or desirable approach. Positive reinforcement, which accentuates rewarding desired behaviors, is generally regarded as a more effective and preferable strategy for behavior management.

★ Punishment and Behavior Modification

Punishment constitutes a technique for altering behavior by administering adverse consequences subsequent to a behavior, aiming to diminish the likelihood of its recurrence. Its objective is to dissuade undesirable behaviors by associating them with negative outcomes.

Various forms of punishment exist, such as verbal admonishments, loss of privileges, time-outs, or physical disciplinary measures, contingent upon the context and severity of the behavior. However, the efficacy of punishment in behavior modification is a topic of debate among psychologists and researchers.

When employed judiciously and sparingly, punishment can yield short-term effects in curbing undesired behaviors. It establishes an immediate correlation between the behavior and the adverse consequence, compelling individuals to reconsider engaging in that behavior to evade similar consequences. Additionally, punishment can function as a deterrent, discouraging individuals from partaking in behaviors that may lead to unfavorable outcomes.

Here's how punishment operates in behavior modification:

- Undesired Behavior: Punishment hinges on an undesired behavior exhibited by an individual, which can encompass any action or response deemed inappropriate, disruptive, or unwanted.

- Aversive Stimulus: Upon the occurrence of the undesired behavior, an aversive stimulus is introduced or a desired stimulus is withdrawn. This aversive stimulus can encompass anything unpleasant or discomforting, like a reprimand, loss of privileges, or physical discomfort.

- Decrease in Behavior: The introduction of the aversive stimulus or the removal of the desired stimulus following the undesired behavior aims to diminish the likelihood of the behavior recurring. The individual links the aversive consequence with the undesired behavior, leading to a reduction in that behavior.

- Learning and Modification: Through repeated encounters with punishment, individuals learn to associate the undesired behavior with negative consequences. This learning process, in turn, modifies behavior by rendering it less probable to occur in the future.

Nonetheless, several limitations and considerations are pertinent when employing punishment as a behavior modification strategy. Primarily, punishment may only transiently suppress behavior without addressing its underlying causes or offering alternative, more desirable behaviors. It fails to instruct individuals on what to do instead of the undesirable behavior, potentially resulting in a resurgence of the unwanted behavior post the removal of the threat of punishment.

Furthermore, punishment can yield unintended repercussions, such as fear, resentment, or learned helplessness. It might strain relationships, impair self-esteem, and engender negative emotional associations. An over-reliance on punishment as a strategy may also foster a focus on avoidance rather than intrinsic motivation, impeding the cultivation of lasting behavior change.

An alternate approach to behavior modification entails reinforcement-based strategies, like positive reinforcement. Positive reinforcement concentrates on fortifying desired behaviors through rewards or positive consequences, enhancing the likelihood of their repetition. It underscores the acknowledgment and promotion of desired behaviors, rather than solely concentrating on penalizing unwanted behaviors.

When resorting to punishment, ethical considerations, fairness, and consistency are paramount. Effective and responsible implementation of punishment as a behavior modification strategy necessitates clear communication, comprehension of the behavioral context, and recognition of individual differences.

Chapter 12

The Law of Self-Concept

The principle known as the Law of Self-Concept asserts that our self-perceptions, beliefs, and evaluations significantly influence our thoughts, emotions, and behaviors. It underscores the pivotal role of our self-concept, which encompasses our beliefs regarding our identity, capabilities, values, and inherent value. This law posits that our self-concept acts as a lens through which we interpret and engage with the world around us, impacting our self-esteem, self-efficacy, and overall sense of worth. Notably, our self-concept is not fixed but can evolve over time through diverse experiences, interactions, and introspection.

The Law of Self-Concept encompasses several key components. Our self-concept is founded on our beliefs and perceptions about ourselves, including aspects like our physical appearance, personality traits, competencies, and the roles we assume in different spheres of life. These factors contribute to our self-image and shape our self-perception. Self-esteem, meanwhile, represents our general assessment of our self-worth, which is influenced by our self-concept and the degree of positivity or negativity in our self-perceptions.

High self-esteem correlates with self-assurance and resilience, while low self-esteem may engender insecurity and negative emotional states. Self-efficacy pertains to our confidence in our capacity to accomplish tasks or achieve objectives, intimately tied to our self-concept and exerting an impact on our motivation and actions. Moreover, our self-concept encompasses our sense of identity and the values that guide us, influencing our decision-making processes and interactions with others.

Furthermore, the Law of Self-Concept includes the concept of self-consistency, reflecting our innate tendency to seek alignment between our self-concept and our thoughts, beliefs, and actions.

Understanding the Law of Self-Concept enables us to grasp the profound influence our self-beliefs exert on our cognitive processes, emotional states, and behavioral patterns. To foster a positive and realistic self-concept, we can cultivate self-awareness, self-acceptance, set achievable goals, and engage in introspection. These practices contribute to enhancing our self-esteem, self-efficacy, and overall psychological well-being.

★ Self-Identity and Behavior

Self-identity serves as a foundational pillar that intricately weaves together the fabric of our behavior, comprising the intricate tapestry of our values, beliefs, and personal attributes that define who we are. This complex interplay between self-identity and behavior illuminates profound insights into how we perceive ourselves and navigate the diverse landscapes of our interactions and choices.

Our self-identity exerts a significant impact on our behavior through various mechanisms:

Behavioral Coherence and Authenticity: Our self-identity acts as a compass, guiding us towards behaviors that resonate with our core beliefs and values. When our actions align with this internal compass, we experience a profound sense of authenticity and harmony. For instance, individuals who identify strongly with environmental stewardship are naturally inclined to engage in eco-conscious behaviors like recycling, reducing waste, and advocating for sustainable practices.

Values as Guiding Lights: Embedded within our self-identity are our deeply held values, the moral compass that directs our decisions and shapes our ethical framework. These values serve as guiding lights, illuminating the path towards behaviors that reflect our principles. For example, a person who values honesty and integrity on a fundamental level is more likely to exhibit truthfulness and ethical conduct in various life situations.

Social Identity Dynamics: Beyond our individual self-identity, we are also influenced by our social identity—the affiliations and groups we belong to, be it cultural, religious, or professional. This social identity shapes our sense of belonging, establishes social norms, and sets expectations that influence our behavior within these collective frameworks.

Self-Perception and Confidence: Our self-identity significantly influences how we perceive ourselves—our strengths, weaknesses, capabilities, and limitations. This self-perception, in turn, impacts our self-efficacy, the belief in our ability to accomplish tasks and achieve goals. For instance, individuals who have a strong self-identity as competent and capable individuals are more likely to take on challenges with confidence and persist in the face of adversity.

Identity-Behavior Nexus: There exists a dynamic feedback loop between our self-identity and behavior. Our actions not only reflect but also reinforce our self-concept. Consistent behaviors that align with our self-identity strengthen our sense of who we are, fostering a deeper connection to our values and beliefs. Conversely, when our behavior contradicts our self-identity, it can trigger cognitive dissonance—a discomfort that motivates us to realign our actions with our self-concept.

By delving into the intricate dance between self-identity and behavior, we gain profound insights into the motivations that drive our actions, the values that underpin our decisions, and the nuanced interplay between our internal beliefs and external expressions. Nurturing a positive and authentic self-identity involves ongoing introspection, acceptance of our evolving selves, and the continual exploration of our values and passions. This journey of self-discovery empowers us to make choices that resonate with our true essence, fostering personal fulfillment, growth, and alignment with our deepest values.

★ Self-Perception and Behavior Alignment

Self-perception and behavior alignment are intertwined elements that shape our decisions and actions. Self-perception is how we view ourselves, including our values, traits, abilities, and beliefs. On the other hand, behavior alignment is the degree to which our behavior is consistent with our self-perception.

When our self-perception and behavior are in alignment, we feel a sense of congruence and genuineness. We act in ways that are in line with our values, beliefs, and self-identity. This alignment has several important effects:

Authenticity: Behavior alignment allows us to be our true selves and live in accordance with our inner values and beliefs. When our behavior reflects our self-perception, we experience a greater sense of authenticity and integrity. This alignment strengthens our connection with ourselves and boosts our overall well-being.

Personal Fulfillment: Engaging in behavior that is in line with our self-perception can lead to personal fulfillment and satisfaction. When we act in ways that are consistent with our beliefs and values, we feel a sense of purpose and meaning. It enables us to live in harmony with our core principles, resulting in greater fulfillment in our lives.

Consistency and Cognitive Dissonance: Behavior alignment helps to maintain internal consistency and reduce cognitive dissonance. Cognitive dissonance occurs when there is a mismatch between our self-perception and our behavior. This inconsistency creates discomfort and motivates us to align our behavior with our self-perception. When our behavior is in alignment, we experience greater harmony and reduce cognitive dissonance.

Goal Pursuit and Motivation: When our behavior is in line with our self-perception, it increases our motivation to pursue goals and aspirations. If we perceive ourselves as competent and capable, we are more likely to engage in behaviors that reflect these qualities and work towards achieving our goals. This alignment reinforces a positive self-perception and strengthens our self-efficacy.

Interpersonal Relationships: Behavior alignment also plays a role in our relationships with others. When our behavior is in line with our self-perception, it enhances our authenticity and fosters genuine connections with others. It allows us to attract and surround ourselves with individuals who resonate with our values and beliefs, contributing to more fulfilling and meaningful relationships.

To promote behavior alignment, it is important to engage in self-reflection, self-awareness, and introspection. By understanding our self-perception, values, and beliefs, we can consciously make choices and engage in behaviors that are consistent with our authentic selves. It may also involve challenging any negative or limiting self-perceptions and developing a growth mindset that allows for self-acceptance and continuous personal development.

★ Self-Concept Development and Change

Self-concept development and change refer to the process of forming and transforming our beliefs, perceptions, and evaluations of ourselves over time. Our self-concept is not fixed but can evolve and adapt through various experiences, interactions, and personal growth.

The formation of self-concept begins in early childhood and continues throughout our lives. It is affected by a variety of factors, including our relationships, cultural and societal influences, successes, failures, feedback from others, and self-reflection. As we progress through different life stages and encounter new situations, our self-concept can undergo significant changes.

Several key elements contribute to self-concept development and change:

Self-Reflection: Engaging in self-reflection and introspection allows us to gain insights into our thoughts, feelings, and beliefs about ourselves. By exploring our values, strengths, weaknesses, and aspirations, we can deepen our understanding of who we are and how we perceive ourselves.

Experiences and Interactions: Our interactions with others and the experiences we have shape our self-concept. Positive experiences, accomplishments, and supportive relationships can enhance our self-perception and self-confidence. On the other hand, challenges, failures, and negative feedback can influence our self-concept by prompting us to re-evaluate our beliefs and make adjustments.

Identity Exploration: Exploring different roles, interests, and identities can contribute to self-concept development. As we engage in various activities, we can gather information about ourselves and learn what resonates with our authentic selves. This exploration allows us to refine and shape our self-concept over time.

Cultural and Societal Influences: Cultural and societal factors also play a role in self-concept development. Our self-perception is affected by the values, norms, and expectations prevalent in our cultural and social environments. These influences shape our beliefs about who we are and the roles we are expected to fulfill.

Lifelong Learning and Growth: Self-concept development is an ongoing process that continues throughout our lives. As we learn new skills, acquire knowledge, and grow as individuals, our self-concept can evolve and expand. Lifelong learning and personal development provide opportunities for self-reflection, challenging limiting beliefs, and embracing new aspects of our identity.

It is important to note that self-concept development is not always a linear progression. It can involve periods of exploration, consolidation, and transformation. Additionally, individual experiences and circumstances can influence the pace and trajectory of self-concept development.

Self-concept change is achievable through intentional efforts and self-awareness. By engaging in practices such as self-reflection, seeking feedback, challenging limiting beliefs, and setting personal goals, we can actively shape and transform our self-concept. Developing a growth mindset, embracing self-acceptance, and fostering a positive self-image can contribute to healthy self-concept development and facilitate personal growth.

Conclusion

Applying the Laws of Human Behavior

Utilizing the profound insights and guiding principles derived from the Laws of Human Behavior opens pathways to a deeper understanding of human interactions, motivations, and behavioral dynamics. The application of these laws extends far beyond mere theoretical understanding; it empowers individuals to foster enriched relationships, make informed decisions, and catalyze personal growth and well-being. Here is a comprehensive exploration of how to intricately apply the Laws of Human Behavior:

Self-Awareness: At the core of effective application lies self-awareness. This entails a continuous process of introspection, where individuals delve into their thoughts, emotions, beliefs, and behavioral patterns. By unraveling these internal aspects, individuals gain profound insights into the underlying drivers of their actions and reactions. Self-awareness serves as a compass, guiding individuals towards conscious choices aligned with their values and aspirations.

Empathy and Understanding: Cultivating empathy is a cornerstone of harmonious interactions. It involves transcending one's own perspective to appreciate and resonate with the experiences, emotions, and viewpoints of others. Through genuine empathy, individuals forge deeper connections, navigate conflicts with sensitivity, and nurture authentic relationships built on mutual understanding and respect.

Positive Reinforcement: The strategic deployment of positive reinforcement fosters a conducive environment for behavioral shaping and enhancement. Recognizing and reinforcing desirable behaviors through meaningful praise, encouragement, and rewards not only strengthens these behaviors but also cultivates a positive and supportive atmosphere conducive to growth and development.

Behavior Modification: Implementing behavior modification strategies requires a nuanced approach. Techniques such as shaping, modeling, and setting clear expectations serve as catalysts for instigating positive behavior change. Breaking down complex goals into manageable steps, providing constructive feedback, and offering support along the journey are integral components of effective behavior modification.

Emotional Intelligence: Mastery of emotional intelligence equips individuals with invaluable tools for navigating interpersonal dynamics. It encompasses self-awareness of one's emotions, effective emotion regulation, and adeptness in perceiving and managing emotions in others. By honing emotional intelligence, individuals enhance their communication skills, build empathy-driven connections, and navigate conflicts with finesse and empathy.

Self-Regulation: The practice of self-regulation empowers individuals to navigate the intricacies of their internal landscape effectively. Techniques such as mindfulness, deep breathing, and cognitive reframing enable individuals to manage impulses, regulate emotions, and respond thoughtfully rather than reactively. Through self-regulation, individuals cultivate emotional resilience and make informed, rational decisions aligned with their long-term goals and values.

Social Influences: A nuanced understanding of social influences sheds light on the complexities of human behavior within societal frameworks. Being mindful of social norms, group dynamics, and conformity pressures allows individuals to navigate social contexts with heightened awareness. This awareness enables individuals to make conscious choices that align with their values while understanding and respecting the diverse perspectives and influences at play.

Personal Growth: The application of the Laws of Human Behavior serves as a catalyst for personal growth and self-improvement. Setting meaningful goals, challenging limiting beliefs, seeking feedback, and embracing a growth mindset are pivotal in this journey. By proactively engaging in self-reflection, learning opportunities, and continuous self-improvement endeavors, individuals unlock their potential and evolve into their best selves.

Ethical Considerations: The ethical application of behavioral principles underscores the importance of integrity, fairness, and respect in all interactions. Upholding ethical standards ensures that interventions and actions prioritize the well-being, autonomy, and dignity of individuals. Ethical considerations form the bedrock of meaningful and sustainable behavioral change and interpersonal interactions.

Lifelong Learning: Embracing a mindset of lifelong learning fuels ongoing growth, curiosity, and adaptability. Continuously seeking new knowledge, exploring diverse perspectives, and staying abreast of evolving behavioral insights enriches individuals' understanding and application of the Laws of Human Behavior. Lifelong learning fuels a perpetual cycle of growth, self-discovery, and transformation.

In essence, the elaborate application of the Laws of Human Behavior transcends theoretical understanding, evolving into a transformative journey of self-discovery, interpersonal harmony, and holistic well-being. Through conscious application and integration of these principles into daily life, individuals unlock their potential, nurture fulfilling relationships, and navigate life's complexities with wisdom and compassion.

Invitation to Explore the Author's Page

Dear Reader,

I hope this message finds you well and inspired by the insights you've gained from reading *"The Laws of Human Behavior"* Your engagement and feedback are invaluable to me as an author, and I would be deeply grateful if you could take a moment to share your thoughts and leave a review on Amazon platform.

Your review not only helps me understand your perspective and areas of interest but also guides other readers in discovering the value and relevance of this book. Your words can inspire and encourage fellow seekers of knowledge to dive into the depths of human behavior and gain new insights into the intricacies of our minds.

Moreover, if you found "*The Laws of Human Behavior*" insightful and enlightening, I invite you to recommend it to your friends, family, colleagues, and anyone who might benefit from understanding the subtle nuances of human psychology. Your recommendation carries weight and can spark meaningful conversations and explorations into the complexities of human nature.

Additionally, I would like to extend an invitation to visit my author's page, where you can explore the other series of this book "*The Basic Laws of human.*" This series delves into the intricate world of human behavior, exploring the underlying principles, fundamentals, and subtle nuances that shape our thoughts, emotions, and actions, offering a structured and comprehensive understanding of our actions, motivations, and interactions.

Furthermore, I have authored other books that might resonate with you and expand your insights into related topics:

- ***Anger Management for Parents with Autistic Kids***

- ***Anger Management for Teens with ADHD***

- ***Dysfunctional Family Signs***

Your support and interest in my work are immensely appreciated, and I look forward to continuing this enriching journey of exploration and discovery together.

With gratitude,

Fanny Hinton

www.ingramcontent.com/pod-product-compliance
Lightning Source LLC
Chambersburg PA
CBHW061630250726
48659CB00004B/1163